**WORKING WITH FAMILIES**

Family Change & Crisis
Workbook

Reproducible Activities to Address the Challenges Families Face Today

By Ester R. A. Leutenberg
& John J. Liptak, Ed.D.

Stress & Wellness Publishers
Duluth, Minnesota

101 W. 2nd St., Suite 203
Duluth, MN 55802

800-247-6789

books@wholeperson.com
www.wholeperson.com

Family Change & Crisis Workbook
Facilitator Reproducible Activities for Groups and Individuals

Copyright ©2015 by Ester R.A. Leutenberg and John J. Liptak. All rights reserved. Except for short excerpts for review purposes and materials in the activities and handouts sections, no part of this book may be reproduced or transmitted in any form by any means, electronic or mechanical without permission in writing from the publisher. Activities and handouts are meant to be photocopied.

All efforts have been made to ensure accuracy of the information contained in this book as of the date published. The author(s) and the publisher expressly disclaim responsibility for any adverse effects arising from the use or application of the information contained herein.

Printed in the United States of America

10 9 8 7 6 5 4 3 2 1

Editorial Director: Carlene Sippola
Art Director: Mathew Pawlak

Library of Congress Control Number: 2015908643
ISBN: 978-157025-332-4

The Cycle of Family Change and Crisis

At some time or another, most families experience changes, then experience stress resulting from the changes, and then go into crisis-mode. However, not all families have a crisis as a result of the stress from change. Resilient families are able to rebound from adversity, to flex in response to the pressures and strains of everyday family life, to become stronger after the change, and to adapt with more resources at their disposal. Resiliency refers to the coping strengths of the individual members, and the combined coping strengths of the family as a whole. Families who exhibit resiliency are flexible when dealing with stress, have coping strengths that can be called upon when experiencing a stressor, and have the ability to reorganize in the face of stress to become stronger and better.

Relationship between Change, Stress, and Crisis

1. CHANGE – The family experiences some type of change. A variety of characteristics will help to determine the extent of the stress that is placed on the family unit.

2. STRESS – Family members experience stress in the forms of fear, anxiety, discomfort, confusion and conflict. The resiliency of family members and the family as a unit will determine the effect of this stress.

3. CRISIS – The stress becomes problematic when it becomes disruptive, or when individual family members begin to show physical and emotional signs of distress.

Types of Family Pressures

Families tend to experience a great deal of stress from both positive and negative events that change their daily lives. As daily life has become more complicated for people in general, the pressures of daily living have tremendously affected the makeup and the coping resources of the family. Here are some (but not all) of the possible types of pressures that can lead to increased stress.

- Abandonment
- Accident
- Addition of a new family member
- Aging
- Break-ups, separation, divorce
- Bullying
- Children in various stages of growth
- Children's/teen's behaviors
- Death
- Disabilities
- Discrimination
- Economic issues
- Emotional abuse
- Empty nest
- Family members serving or coming back from serving one's country
- Financial losses
- Housing issues
- Incarceration
- Job insecurity
- Mental health issues
- Natural disasters
- Neighbors' complaints or behavior
- New place to live
- Physical abuse
- Physical health issues
- PTSD
- Runaways
- Substance abuse
- Suicidal thoughts
- Survivors of a loved one who died by suicide
- Terrorism
- Theft
- Unemployment
- Unexpected pregnancy
- Usual disappointments (not making the cheerleading team, not receiving a promotion, etc.)
- Usual events (graduations, weddings, prom, concerts, ball games)
- Verbal abuse
- Veteran homecoming/readjustment
- Violence
- Workplace pressures
- And so many more!

Because of these daily strains, stress has become a natural part of each family's daily life. At one point in time, family units were viewed as relatively stress-free and the family structure was seen as a safe haven from all everyday stressors. Unfortunately, families face many different unique problems that can be stressful. All families experience stress as a result of change, but this stress need not end in a crisis. The impact of this change is dependent upon each family member's perception of stressor, as well as their ability to cope with the stressor both as individuals and as members of a family unit.

With any types of change and crisis in a family comes a certain amount of stress. Family stress can be defined as any sort of worry or tension about the family status quo. Stress or tension can be caused by life transitions (empty-nest syndrome), events (birth of a child), and external forces (war, unemployment, and terrorism). Positive life transitions, events and forces are often perceived by the family as inevitable and normal (and even desirable), thus the family accepts the transition or event, and develops, matures and changes to adapt to the new situation. On the other hand, negative life transitions, events, and forces are problematic for a family and create stress for the family system. When change becomes overly problematic, it elevates the level of stress in the family, and family members or the family as a whole becomes dissatisfied, stressed, and family members begin to show symptoms of disruption.

Societal Factors

It will serve us well if we explore the sources and effects of stress that occur. Some of the societal factors that have been linked to causing an elevation of the level of family stress include:
- An increase in the amount of people suffering from Post-Traumatic Stress Disorder (PTSD).
- An increase in the lack of religion and/or spirituality in the family system.
- An increase in the number of natural disasters with which families are forced to cope.
- An increase in stress as a result of having to care for an individual with a long-term illness or disability.
- An increase in the stress resulting from caring for elderly parents.
- An increase in the demands created by the need to balance work and family responsibilities.
- An increase in technology has made being available 24/7 a reality for many working people. This increased need to be available to employers has caused an increase of stress among working professionals.

What Happens in the Family?

Although the terms stress and crisis are often used interchangeably, there are distinctions between the two. Stress occurs when there is a change in the family's equilibrium due to a stressor. Stress, in and of itself, can either be positive and motivating (eustress), or negative (distress). Stress becomes problematic when it reaches a level at which the family becomes disrupted, or when individual family members become dissatisfied and/or begin to show the physical and emotional signs of distress. Levels of stress are often determined by the adequacy of family resources to cope and adapt to the stress.

Crisis occurs when the disruption or disturbance in family equilibrium becomes so overwhelming, severe or acute, that the family is unable to cope or adapt, and the family system becomes blocked and unable to function. Therefore, when a family is in crisis, it no longer functions efficiently or effectively; family roles and tasks may not be performed adequately; boundaries break down; emotions rise; and individual family members no longer function at their best levels.

Some characteristics of a family in crisis:
- The event preceding the crisis is perceived as threatening to the family.
- The family is unable to modify or reduce the impact of the stressful event.
- Fear, tension, and/or confusion increases.
- A high level of discomfort is evident.
- A state of disequilibrium is followed by the transition to a crisis.

Many attempts have been made to try to determine the intensity of a stressor on family members and the family as a system. While no definitive system has been developed, family stressors and crises are often categorized by responses to the following dimensions:
1) Where is the source of the stress? Is it internal or external to the family system?
2) Does the stress affect certain parts of the system or the entire family system?
3) What is the severity of the stress?
4) Does the stress present a long-term or short-term problem?
5) Was the stress expected and predicted, or not?
6) Did the stress occur because of natural conditions within the family unit or was it created by other people?
7) Does the stress mean that there will be a shortage of human resources or material resources?
8) Is the stress open to reversal or some level of resolution?
9) Can the stress be categorized as political, economic, spiritual/religious, health-related, career related, economic, moral, or sexual, or some combination of these categories?
10) Were the family members prepared ahead of time or was the event or situation a shock?

Family Coping Strategies

Families must find ways to cope with stress as family team members and as individuals. Coping is a process by which family members achieve balance in the family system so that it promotes growth and development. Coping means actively managing stress that could grow significantly more extreme over time.

When families begin to experience stress that can potentially become a crisis, they must rely on a variety of coping resources and mechanisms:

- **Cognitive Strategies** present ways that individual family members can alter their perceptions of stressful events. Strategies include reframing the problem, thinking positively, and looking at negative and irrational thinking.
- **Direct Action** guides each person to acquire a new set of resources to help individual family members cope with stress. Strategies include learning new skills, getting direct help or support, and acquiring needed resources.
- **Controlling Emotions** teaches ways to regulate the feelings generated by the stressor before it becomes a crisis.
- **Management of Family Life** teaches management of various dimensions of family life while at the same time including the following strategies:
    Maintaining effective family communication
    Preserving the family organization
    Promoting family member interdependence
    Ensuring family member self-esteem
    Maintaining family bonds for unity
    Developing and maintaining social supports
    Attempting to control, as much as possible, the impact of stressors and the amount of change in the family structure.
- **Adaptation** shows ways to recover from stress and/or crisis. Strategies include altering the internal family rules, roles and perceptions to better achieve a family-environment fit.
- **Developing Strategies** to be resilient in the face of change.

In order to maintain an effective and useful family unit, family members must develop skills for managing change, coping with stress, and building resiliency from external and internal stressors.

The *Family Change & Crisis Workbook* provides assessments and self-guided activities to help family members explore old patterns of interaction and behavior that are no longer effective, and to identify ways to develop more effective interactions and behaviors. Many choices of self-exploration assessments and activities are provided for family members to use collaboratively with other family members to develop a healthy family unit.

As families work through the activities in this workbook,
it might be helpful to add a scrapbook to collect pictures drawn by participants,
photos collected, completed activities, and dated family scores to
demonstrate connectedness which may grow through the use of the
Family Change & Crisis Workbook

Introduction

The *Family Change & Crisis Workbook* Contents

The *Family Change & Crisis Workbook* contains the materials facilitators need to work with changes that cause stress and possibly a crisis in the family unit.

Each chapter contains six primary elements:
1) A set of skills to be gained from completion of the assessments and activities by all family members.
2) A set of assessments to help children/teens gather information about themselves in a focused situation.
3) A set of assessments to help children/teens gather their perceived information about how the other family members feel in a shared and focused situation.
4) A set of assessments to help caregiver adults gather information about themselves in a focused situation.
5) A set of assessments to help caregiver adults gather their perceived information about how the other family members feel in a shared focused situation.
6) A set of guided self-exploration activities to help all of the participants to process information and learn ways to build a stronger family unit.

Assessments are valuable tools for facilitators to use with family members to build a healthy family unit:
- Understand and predict future behavior
- Identify the nature of problems and explore possible solutions
- Explore the family as a system, rather than focusing on individual behavior
- Identify the family constructs, patterns, structure, and level of functioning
- Develop hypotheses (with the help of the facilitator) about the issues most often interfering with positive family dynamics
- Explore family members' perceptions of the various issues affecting their family
- Identify their areas of strength as a family

Therefore, through the assessment process, facilitators will be better able to join with the family members, provide support, offer feedback, validate issues and concerns, understand and appreciate each other's perceptions and feelings, enhance family strengths, and generate hope for the future.

Assessments in Each Chapter

Family members often need to work together on issues they are experiencing in their household. However, before effective, therapeutic discussions can take place, family members need vehicles with which they can explore and categorize their thinking about their current family life. Assessments are a valuable method for collecting important information about members of a family and can provide a vehicle with which family members can tell their narratives safely. Assessments also provide family members and the facilitator with different perspectives held by various family members. Therefore, assessments are included for facilitators to use in examining family relationships, functions, constructs and dynamics.

Each chapter of this workbook begins with four different reproducible assessments, scoring instructions, and interpretation guides that can be easily used with all members of the family with whom you are working. As the facilitator, you may choose to use any combination of assessments that represent the family dynamics of your current clients. You may choose to use one scale or all of them, depending on the make-up of the family and the number of people in the family with whom you are working.

Photocopy as many pages of each as you need for each participant.

(Continued on the next page)

The *Family Change & Crisis Workbook* Contents *(Continued)*

The scales related to the topics covered in each chapter will include the following:

Assessment #1: One assessment for each child to identity personal feelings about the stressful changes occurring in the family.

Assessment #2: One assessment for each child to identify perceptions of one or more of the children's/teens' caregivers: (parent, grandparent, relative, group parent, etc.) about the stressful changes in the family. Each member's perceptions of the others' feelings are vitally important for them to understand and empathize with them.

Assessment #3: One assessment for each adult (children's/teens' caregivers: parent, grandparent, relative, group parent, etc.) to identity their own feelings about the stressful changes in the family.

Assessment #4: One assessment for each adult (children's/teens' caregivers: parent, grandparent, relative, group parent, etc.) to identify perceptions of each child about the stressful changes in the family. Each member's perceptions of the others' feeling are vitally important for them to understand and empathize with them.

Assessments are critical in working with families experiencing change, stress, and maybe even crisis. The assessments contained in this workbook provide family members with valuable information about themselves and their perceptions of each other. Assessments in this workbook are different from traditional assessments because they are designed for all members of the family, not just the adults or just the teens.

Quantitative vs. Qualitative Assessments

This book contains *qualitative self-assessments* and not *quantitative tests*. Qualitative assessments derive specialized, focused information about family members and family dynamics.

1) These qualitative assessments help identify patterns of behavior and attitudes which are productive and unproductive in a family setting. The purpose of these assessments is not to find fault with any family members; the assessments are designed to guide self-discovery and inform family members.

2) Quantitative assessments measure knowledge or right or wrong responses. These qualitative assessments are designed to help family members explore their current family dynamics, not yield right or wrong answers. These assessments ask only for opinions or attitudes about topics related to their family life.

3) Quantitative assessments often have formal ways for family members to compare their scores with others who have taken the same assessments. These qualitative assessments are based on self-reported data. In other words, the accuracy and usefulness of the information is dependent on the information that participants honestly provide about themselves. All scores will simply be compared with the scores of other members of the family.

4) Quantitative assessments are designed to be administered by the facilitator. The qualitative assessments in this workbook are designed to be administered, scored, and interpreted by the participants, with the help of the facilitator, as a starting point for them to begin to learn more about themselves and their behavior within the family structure. Remind participants that the assessments are exploratory exercises and not a final measurement of functioning.

When family members are completing, scoring and interpreting the assessments contained in this workbook, please be aware that the assessments are not a substitute for professional assistance. If you feel any of the members of the family with which you are working need more assistance than you can provide, please refer them to an appropriate professional.

(Continued on the next page)

Introduction

The *Family Change & Crisis Workbook* Contents *(Continued)*

Guided Self-Exploration Activities

Guided self-exploration activities assist all family members in self-reflection to identify effective family behaviors as well as ineffective family behaviors. Guided self-exploration is designed to help family members make a series of discoveries about themselves and other members of the family. These insights will help family members realize that a family is much more than the sum of its individual parts.

These brief, easy-to-use self-reflection tools are designed to promote insight and self-growth. The activities in this workbook are also related to the assessments so that you can identify and select activities quickly and easily. Many different types of guided self-exploration activities are provided for you to pick and choose the activities most needed by your family members and that will be most appealing to them.

> **The GUIDED-SELF-EXPLORATION ACTIVITIES can take TWO DISTINCT FORMS:**
> 1. Writing, list-making and journaling activities for **adults, older children and teens**. These types of activities allow older family members to be introspective and write about their experiences..
> 2. Any of the handouts can be adapted by the facilitator for use with **children or teens (depending on their age and/or maturity level)** by asking them to draw, doodle, or respond about the situation represented on the handout. This will allow an opportunity for them to express themselves in ways they are able.

The unique features of self-guided exploration activities make them usable and appropriate for a variety of individual sessions and family sessions.

Features of Guided Self-Exploration Activities

- **Quick, easy and rewarding to use** – These guided self-exploration activities are designed to be an efficient, appealing method for motivating family members to explore information about themselves - including their thoughts, feelings, actions and relationships - in a relatively short period of time.
- **Reproducible** – Because the guided self-exploration activities can be reproduced by the facilitator, no more than one book needs to be purchased. You may photocopy as many items as you wish for your participants. If you want to add or delete words on a page, make one photocopy, white out and/or write your own words, and then make photocopies from your personalized master.
- **Participative** – These guided self-exploration activities help family members to quickly focus their attention, aid them in the self-reflection process, and guide them to learn new and more effective ways of interacting with each other.
- **Motivating to complete** – Because they can be completed by all members of the family, the guided self-exploration activities are designed to help all family members feel empowered to face the issues confronting the family and to learn ways for the family to be a more cohesive unit.
- **User-friendly** – The guided self-exploration activities are user-friendly, and family members will feel motivated and self-empowered after completing these activities.
- **Adaptable to a variety of family situations and dynamics** – The guided self-exploration activities can be used with a variety of today's families and can be tailored to meet the needs of the families with whom you work.
- **Focused** – Each guided self-exploration activity is designed to focus on a single set of coping issues that families typically face.
- **Flexible** – The guided self-exploration activities are flexible and can be used independently or to supplement other types of interventions.

Family Change & Crisis Workbook

The Working with Family Series

As the structure of families has changed, so has the need for new tools, techniques and resources with which facilitators can assist family members.

The purpose of this new series of workbooks is to help practitioners who work with families in need of help/intervention to have a tool for identifying family members' issues through qualitative assessments as well as activities designed to overcome these problems.

This workbook series is unique in that all of the assessments and activities are designed for all members of the family, not exclusively for children, for teens, or for adults.

The assessments and activities in this workbook and others in this series will allow family members to accomplish the following:

- Know, understand and empathize with each other better, and accept and celebrate differences in family members. This will provide family members the tools they need to work together to blend more effectively.

- Develop a greater feeling of bonding and interacting in positive ways, with the common goal that family members genuinely care for one another in nurturing ways.

- Accept each individual family member as a unique and special person.

- Provide support and comfort to each other to enhance a sense of trust, loyalty and respect for each other.

- Communicate honestly with each other, resolve conflicts, and compromise and negotiate for their desires and needs.

~~~~~~

The next page is for your participants!

As they are ready to begin the assessments in this workbook, it is necessary to convey to the participants the instructions on the page, *For the Participants.* **(page xi)**

- **You may read it to the participants.**
- **They can read it to themselves.**
- **You may photocopy one for each participant.**
- **Different volunteers can read each bullet point aloud.**

Introduction

For the Participants

**You are about to start a new adventure,
to learn more about yourself, your family and your home life.
You will use assessments and self-exploration activities.**

- Because there is no time limit for completing the assessments, you can work at your own pace. Allow yourself time to reflect on your results: how they compare to what you already know about yourself, and what other family members have said about you.

- Other members of your family may be taking the same or similar assessments. Some assessments are designed to help you explore your feelings about your family life, and some will ask for your perceptions of other family members. *(How you are aware of, understand, or interpret the thoughts, feelings, and actions of these family members.)*

- Do not answer the assessments as you think other family members would like you to answer them. These assessments are for your personal reflections on your family life and to help you to explore some issues that may be keeping your family from being as close, comfortable and content as you can all be.

- Assessments are powerful tools, but only if you are honest with yourself. Take your time and be truthful in your responses so that your results are an honest reflection of you. Your level of commitment in completing the assessment honestly will determine how much you learn about yourself and your home environment.

- If you are going to complete two assessments, be sure to read the instructions. The assessments have similar formats, but they have different scales, responses, scoring instructions, and methods for interpretation.

- Remember that learning about yourself in your home and family life, as well as in relation to other members of your family, is designed to promote your growth as well as the growth of everyone in your family unit.

Enjoy taking the assessments and discovering your results.

*Respond in an honest and open way.
It may sometimes be difficult to admit the truth, or hear the truth from someone else,
but an open forum for communication is part of the process
to learn as much about yourself and your home/family environment as you can.*

Chapter Topics

The *Family Change & Crisis Workbook* is designed to be used either independently or as part of an integrated curriculum. You may administer any of the assessments and the guided self-exploration activities to an individual or multiple family members with whom you are working, or you may administer any of the activities over multiple sessions. Feel free to pick and choose those assessments and activities that best lead to the outcomes you desire. The assessments and activities are divided into four chapters to help you identify and select assessments easily and quickly.

Chapter I: Family Changes
This chapter helps family members explore the types and intensity of the stressful changes the family is currently going through.

Chapter II: Family Crisis
This chapter helps family members explore how difficult a change can be on some or all family members and ways to manage and cope with issues and crises.

Chapter III: Family Stress
This chapter helps family members explore how well they are managing their current family stress and explore ways to cope more effectively with change and stress.

Chapter IV: Family Resilience
This chapter helps family members explore ways that the family can come together and build resilience as a family after stressful changes and crises.

Thanks to these professionals who make us look good!

Editorial Director	–	Carlene Sippola
Cover Design & Art Director	–	Mathew Pawlak
Editor and Lifelong Teacher	–	Eileen Regen, M.Ed., CJE
Reviewer and Proofreader	–	Jay Leutenberg, CASA
Reviewer and Behavioral Skills Expert	–	Carol Butler, MS Ed, RN, C
Reviewer and Family Therapy Expert	–	Selma Gwatkin, MA, LIMFT
Reviewer and Teen Counselor/Teacher	–	Niki Tilicki, MAED

Table of Contents – **Introduction**

The Cycle of Family Change, Stress, and Crisis iii

Types of Family Changes that Lead to Stress and Crisis iv

Societal Changes. v

What Happens in the Family? v

Coping with Stress as a Family vi

The *Family Changes, Stress & Crisis Workbook* Contents – vii

    Six Primary Elements vii

    Assessments are Valuable Tools vii

    Assessments in Each Chapter vii

    Assessments: viii

        Quantitative vs Qualitative Assessments ix

        Guided Self-Exploration Activities ix

        Guided Self-Exploration Activities – Two Distinct Forms ix

        Features of Guided Self-Exploration Activities ix

The *Working with Family Issues* Series x

For the Participants. xi

Chapter Topics xii

Our Thanks xii

Table of Contents: Introduction xiii

Table of Contents: Chapter 1 – Family Changes xiv

Table of Contents: Chapter 2 – Family Stress. xv

Table of Contents: Chapter 3 – Family Crisis. xvi

Table of Contents: Chapter 4 – Family Resiliency xvii

Chapter I – Family Changes

For the Facilitator – Explanation of the Four Scales in this Chapter..........19

Family Changes Skills 20

Family Changes Scale Introductions and Directions 21

Scale #1 – Child's/Teen's Family Changes..........22

Scale #1 – Scale Scoring Directions, Profile Interpretation and Individual Scale Descriptions 23

Scale #2 – Child's/Teen's Perception of an Adult's *Family Changes* 24

Scale #2 – Scale Scoring Directions, Profile Interpretation and Individual Scale Descriptions 25

Scale #3 – Adult's *Family Changes*..........26

Scale #3 – Scale Scoring Directions, Profile Interpretation and Individual Scale Descriptions 27

Scale #4 – Adult's Perception of a Child's/Teen's *Family Changes* 28

Scale #4 – Scale Scoring Directions, Profile Interpretation and Individual Scale Descriptions 29

Family Changes Scale – Family Score Totals 30

Our Family's Stressors..........31

The Story of Our Change 32

In the Midst of Change 33

Processing the Family Change 34-35

Impacting the Stressors of Change 36

My Worries..........37

Logical or Illogical Thoughts?..........38

ME – Before & After the Change..........39

US – Before & After the Change 40

What Do I Look Like? 41

Introduction

Chapter II – **Family Crisis**

For the Facilitator – Explanation of the Four Scales in this Chapter 43

Family Crisis Skills. 44

Family Crisis Scale Introduction & Directions 45

Scale #1 – Child's/Teen's *Family Crisis* 46

Scale #1 – Scale Scoring Directions, Profile Interpretation and Individual Scale Descriptions 47

Scale #2 – Child's/Teen's Perception of the Adult's *Family Crisis*. 48

Scale #2 – Scale Scoring Directions, Profile Interpretation and Individual Scale Descriptions 49

Scale #3 – Adult's *Family Crisis* – Scale Scoring Directions. 50

Scale #3 – Scale Scoring Directions, Profile Interpretation and Individual Scale Descriptions 51

Scale #4 – Adult's Perception of a Child's/Teen's *Family Crisis* 52

Scale #4 – Scale Scoring Directions, Profile Interpretation and Individual Scale Descriptions 53

Family Crisis – Family Score Totals. 54

Processing a Change Situation 55-58

Let's Discuss It! 59

Withdrawing 60

Problems. 61

Tension. 62

Ways I'm Critical 63

Negative and Positive Emotions 64

Expressing How You Feel 65

Stuck in Negative Feelings 66

Guilt about the Family Change 67

Dear Journal 68

Chapter III – **Family Stress**

For the Facilitator – Explanation of the Four Scales in this Chapter 69

Family Stress Skills 70

Family Stress Scale Introduction & Directions 71

Scale #1 – Child's/Teen's *Family Stress* 72

Scale #1 – Scale Scoring Directions, Profile Interpretation and Individual Scale Descriptions 73

Scale #2 – Child's/Teen's Perception of the Adult's *Family Stress* 74

Scale #2 – Scale Scoring Directions, Profile Interpretation and Individual Scale Descriptions 75

Scale #3 – Adult's *Family Stress* – Scale Scoring Directions 76

Scale #3 – Scale Scoring Directions, Profile Interpretation and Individual Scale Descriptions 77

Scale #4 – Adult's Perception of a Child's/Teen's *Family Stress* 78

Scale #4 – Scale Scoring Directions, Profile Interpretation and Individual Scale Descriptions 79

Family Stress Scale – Family Score Totals 80

Unhealthy Ways to Manage Stress 81

The Trouble with Lying 82

Learn to Forgive 83

Fight Fairly 84

Family Enjoyment 85

Reducing Stress 86

Support 87

Writing a Letter 88

What is in My Control and What Isn't 89

My Fears about Our Future 90

Appreciation 91

Playing the Blame Game 92

Reframe Problems 93

New Routines 94

Four Step Family Problem Solving 95-96

Chapter IV – **Family Resilience**

For the Facilitator – Explanation of the Four Scales in this Chapter............97

Family Resilience Skills...............98

Scale Introduction & Directions...............99

Scale #1 – Child's/Teen's *Family Resilience* 100

Scale #1 – Scale Scoring Directions, Profile Interpretation and Individual Scale Descriptions.....101

Scale #2 – Child's/Teen's Perception of the Adult's *Family Resilience*...............102

Scale #2 – Scale Scoring Directions, Profile Interpretation and Individual Scale Descriptions.....103

Scale #3 – Adult's *Family Resilience* – Scale Scoring Directions...............104

Scale #3 – Scale Scoring Directions, Profile Interpretation and Individual Scale Descriptions.....105

Scale #4 – Adult's Perception of a Child's/Teen's *Family Resilience* 106

Scale #4 – Scale Scoring Directions, Profile Interpretation and Individual Scale Descriptions.....107

Family Resilience Scale – Family Score Totals...............108

The Family That Works Together 109

Family Strengths...............110

Optimistic People...............111

Positive Mottos...............112

Learn to Forgive 113

Share Meals Together 114

enCOURAGEment 115

Daily Reminders...............116

Kindness Re-examined 117

Interests 118

Family Events 119

Looking at the Big Picture 120

Respect...............121

Our Family's Strengths 122

CHAPTER 1

Family Changes

For the Facilitator

Explanation of the four scales in this chapter

As the facilitator, you may choose any combination of assessments that will work for each of the particular families with whom you are working.

You may choose to use one scale or all of them,
depending on the make-up of the family and the number of people in the family.

Photocopy as many of each as needed.

1. **One for each child/teen** to identity personal feelings

2. **One for each child/teen** to identify perceptions of adults' feelings

3. **One for each adult** to identity personal feelings

4. **One for each adult** to identify perceptions of children's or teens' feelings

**You will need to photocopy the corresponding
Introduction and Directions
for each scale you administer.**

Chapter I – *Family Changes* Skills

These skills are behavioral objectives which family members will meet as they engage in the assessments and guided self-exploration activities.

Children/Teens
Identify own thoughts, feelings and behaviors related to their family's changes and their perceptions of one or more adults' thoughts, feelings and behaviors in the family setting by responding to twenty prompts.

Adults
Identify own thoughts, feelings and behaviors related to family's changes and their perceptions of one or more children/teens' thoughts, feelings and behaviors in the family setting by responding to twenty prompts.
Process the change by journaling about:
    How the stress from the change affects certain members or the entire family.
    The gradual or unexpected onset of the change and stress.
    How adults are/are not coping.
    Who helps members manage stress, how, and ways to obtain additional assistance.

All Family Members
- Assess *Family Changes* scores as low, moderate or high on the *Scale Profile Interpretation*.
- Identify their scores' meanings based on the *Scale Profile Interpretation* and *Scale Description*.
- Compare their perceptions by entering scores onto a *Family Changes Scale*.
- Identify and explain change-related stressors from forty-two issues, plus others.
- Describe changes, stress, and disrupted family dynamics.
- Evaluate a current change, and the effectiveness of either changing or avoiding the issue.
- Name a person with whom to discuss family change issues.
- Describe the change and each family member's role in the stress.
- Identify how each member reacts to change, and how each can help reduce the stress for others.
- Document six worries, the personal and family effects, and with whom to process concerns.
- Categorize four thoughts about the change as logical or illogical and explain.
- Name a person who can help sort out the nature of the thoughts.
- Describe self before and after the family change and note positive and negative differences.
- Describe the family before and after the change and note positive and negative differences.
- Depict self as stressed, and then as calm.
- State when one looks like the "stressed out" picture and when one looks calm.

Family Changes Scale
Introduction & Directions

It is important to explore how each of the individual family members feel after a stressful change and to also explore how family members perceive how the other family members feel. Everyone, at some time, experiences change in their lives, and they all deal with it in different ways with varying degrees of success.

This scale can help you explore how well you are handling the stress of change that is happening in your family, as well as how you feel the others are handling it. This scale contains 20 statements. Read each of the statements and decide how descriptive each statement is of you or your family member. In each of the choices listed, circle the number of your response on the line to the right of each statement.

Examples

Scale # 1 and # 3 (Individual's responses)

In the following example, the circled number 1 under "FALSE" indicates the statement is not true of the person completing the scale.

Regarding our family changes   TRUE   FALSE
   Little things are starting to bother me. . . . . .2 . . . .(1)

Scale # 2 and # 4: (Individual's perceptions)

In the following example, the circled number 2 under "TRUE" indicates the person who is completing the scale believes that this statement is true about the other family member.

Regarding our family changes, I believe this adult...   TRUE   FALSE
   is bothered by little things. . . . .(2) 1

This is not a test and there are no right or wrong answers. Do not spend too much time thinking about your answers. Your initial response will be the most true for you. Be sure to respond to every statement.

(Turn to the next page and begin.)

Family Change & Crisis Workbook

SCALE #1
Child's/Teen's *Family Changes*

Child's/Teen's Name _____ Date _____

Regarding our family changes	TRUE	FALSE
Little things are starting to bother me.	2	1
I have frequent fights with other family members.	2	1
I don't feel like I'm getting the support I need	2	1
I feel like life is hopeless.	2	1
I rarely lash out at other people	1	2
I don't want to be around other family members	2	1
I often feel short-tempered	2	1
I am often fearful even when there is nothing to fear	2	1
I rarely get depressed about anything	1	2
I have been sleeping about eight hours a night	1	2
I often catch myself verbally attacking others	2	1
My appetite has remained the same.	1	2
I often have a strong urge to just run away	2	1
I am excited to get up in the mornings	1	2
I often feel like crying for no reason.	2	1
I feel tired a lot of the time	2	1
I have not experienced chest pain or my heart racing	1	2
I often have an upset stomach.	2	1
I feel anxious a lot of the time.	2	1
I find myself biting my fingernails a lot	2	1

TOTAL = _____

Family Changes

SCALE #1
Child's/Teen's *Family Changes*
Scale Scoring Directions

Name _____ Date _____

The scale you just completed is designed to measure if and how the family changes are distressing you.
For the items on the previous page, count the scores you circled.
Put that total on the line marked TOTAL at the end of the scale.
Then, transfer your total to the space below.

My Family Change   Total = _____

Scale Profile Interpretation

Scale Score	Result	Indications
20 to 26	Low	Low scores indicate that you are not very distressed by the changes. You are doing a great job of coping.
27 to 33	Moderate	Moderate scores indicate that you are being somewhat distressed by the changes in your family. You are doing a pretty good job of coping.
34 to 40	High	High scores indicate that you are extremely distressed by the changes in your family. You are not doing a great job of coping.

Individual Scale Descriptions

My Family Change – The child or teen scoring high on this scale is very distressed relating to the changes in the family, allows small things to be bothersome, becomes angry with others easily, may be experiencing some depression, is not sleeping well, feels tired, and may be crying a lot of the time.

Family Change & Crisis Workbook

SCALE #2
Child's/Teen's Perception of an Adult's *Family Changes*

Child's/Teen's Name _____

Adult's Name _____ Date _____

Regarding our family changes, I believe this adult …	TRUE	FALSE
is bothered by little things.	2	1
has frequent fights with other family members	2	1
doesn't feel supported by others.	2	1
seems to feel like life is hopeless.	2	1
rarely lashes out at other people.	1	2
doesn't want to be around other family members.	2	1
is often short-tempered.	2	1
is often fearful even when there is nothing to fear.	2	1
rarely get depressed about anything.	1	2
has been sleeping the whole night.	1	2
often verbally attacks others.	2	1
has the same appetite as always.	1	2
seems to have a strong urge to just run away	2	1
is excited to get up in the mornings.	1	2
often cries for no reason.	2	1
looks tired a lot of the time.	2	1
has not complained of chest pain or heart racing	1	2
often has an upset stomach	2	1
is worried a lot of the time	2	1
bites fingernails a lot	2	1

TOTAL = _____

Family Changes

SCALE #2
Child's/Teen's Perception of One Adult's *Family Changes* Scale Scoring Directions

Child's/Teen's Name _____

Adult's Name _____ Date _____

The scale you just completed is designed to measure how you perceive the family changes are distressing the above stated adult.
For the items on the previous page, count the scores you circled.
Put that total on the line marked TOTAL at the end of the scale.
Then, transfer your total to the space below.

My Family Change   Total = _____

Scale Profile Interpretation

Scale Score	Result	Indications
20 to 26	Low	Low scores indicate that you perceive that the above stated adult is not very distressed by the changes and/or is doing a great job of coping.
27 to 33	Moderate	Moderate scores indicate that you perceive that the above stated adult is somewhat distressed by the changes in your family and/or is doing a pretty good job of coping.
34 to 40	High	High scores indicate that you perceive that the above stated adult is very distressed by the changes in your family and/or is not doing a good job of coping.

Individual Scale Descriptions

My Family Change – The child or teen scoring high on this scale indicates a perception that this above stated adult is very distressed by the changes in the family, allows small things to be bothersome, becomes angry with others easily, may be experiencing some depression, is not sleeping well, feels tired, and may be crying a lot of the time.

SCALE #3
Adult's *Family Changes*

Adult's Name _____ Date _____

Regarding our family changes ...	**TRUE**	**FALSE**
Little things are starting to bother me.	2	1
I have frequent fights with other family members.	2	1
I don't feel like I'm getting the support I need	2	1
I feel like life is hopeless.	2	1
I rarely lash out at other people	1	2
I don't want to be around other family members	2	1
I often feel short-tempered	2	1
I am often fearful even when there is nothing to fear	2	1
I rarely get depressed about anything	1	2
I have been sleeping about eight hours a night	1	2
I often catch myself verbally attacking others	2	1
My appetite has remained the same.	1	2
I often have a strong urge to leave.	2	1
I am excited to get up in the mornings	1	2
I often feel like crying for no reason.	2	1
I feel tired a lot of the time	2	1
I have not experienced chest pain or my heart racing	1	2
I often have an upset stomach.	2	1
I feel anxious a lot of the time.	2	1
I find myself biting my fingernails a lot	2	1

TOTAL = _____

Family Changes

SCALE #3
Adult's *Family Changes*
Scale Scoring Directions

Adult's Name _____ Date _____

The scale you just completed is designed to measure if and how the family changes are distressing you.
For the items on the previous page, count the scores you circled.
Put that total on the line marked TOTAL at the end of the scale.
Then, transfer your total to the space below.

My Family Change   Total = _____

Scale Profile Interpretation

Scale Score	Result	Indications
20 to 26	Low	Low scores indicate that you are not very distressed by the changes. You are doing a great job of coping.
27 to 33	Moderate	Moderate scores indicate that you are being somewhat distressed by the changes in your family. You are doing a pretty good job of coping.
34 to 40	High	High scores indicate that you are extremely distressed by the changes in your family. You are not doing a great job of coping.

Individual Scale Descriptions

My Family Change – The adult scoring high on this scale is very distressed by the changes in the family, allows small things to be bothersome, becomes angry with others easily, may be experiencing some depression, is not sleeping well, feels tired and may be crying a lot of the time.

Family Change & Crisis Workbook

SCALE #4
Adult's Perception of a Child's/Teen's *Family Changes*

Adult's Name _____

Child's/Teen's Name _____ Date _____

Regarding our family changes, I believe this child or teen …	TRUE	FALSE
is bothered by little things.	2	1
has frequent fights with other family members	2	1
doesn't feel supported by others	2	1
seems to feel like life is hopeless	2	1
rarely lashes out at other people	1	2
doesn't want to be around other family members	2	1
is often short-tempered	2	1
is often fearful even when there is nothing to fear.	2	1
rarely get depressed about anything	1	2
has been sleeping the whole night.	1	2
often verbally attacks others.	2	1
has the same appetite as always	1	2
seems to have a strong urge to just run away	2	1
is excited to get up in the mornings	1	2
often cries for no reason.	2	1
looks tired a lot of the time	2	1
has not complained of chest pain or heart racing	1	2
often has an upset stomach	2	1
is worried a lot of the time	2	1
bites fingernails a lot	2	1

TOTAL = _____

Family Changes

SCALE #4
Adult's Perception of a Child's/Teen's *Family Changes*
Scale Scoring Directions

Adult's Name _____

Child's/Teen's Name _____ Date _____

The scale you just completed is designed to measure how you perceive the family changes are distressing the above stated child or teen.
For the items on the previous page, count the scores you circled.
Put that total on the line marked TOTAL at the end of the scale.
Then, transfer your total to the space below.

My Family Change   Total = _____

Scale Profile Interpretation

Scale Score	Result	Indications
20 to 26	Low	Low scores indicate that you perceive that the above stated child or teen is not very distressed by the changes and/or is doing a great job of coping
27 to 33	Moderate	Moderate scores indicate that you perceive that the above stated child or teen is somewhat distressed by the changes in your family and/or is doing a pretty good job of coping.
34 to 40	High	High scores indicate that you perceive that this child or teen is very distressed by the changes in your family and/or not doing a good job of coping.

Individual Scale Descriptions

My Family Change – The adult scoring high on this scale indicates a perception that this above stated child or teen is very distressed by the changes in the family, allows small things to be bothersome, becomes angry with others easily, may be experiencing some depression, is not sleeping well, feels tired and may be crying a lot of the time.

Family Changes Scale
Family Score Totals

Insert everyone's name who completed each scale and write their scale scores.
This form can be helpful in allowing family members to compare their own results.

Scale 1 Name (Child's/Teen's Scale)	Total Score
(example) Bill	36

Scale 2 Name (Child's/Teen's Perception of Adult Scale)	Total Score

Scale 3 Name (Adult's Scale)	Total Score

Scale 4 Name (Adult's Perception of Child's/Teen's Scale)	Total Score

Family Changes

Our Family's Stressors Due to Change

Place a check in the box for each issue in your family. Next to it, briefly explain.

- ☐ Abandonment _____
- ☐ Abuse _____
- ☐ Accident _____
- ☐ Aging _____
- ☐ Arguments _____
- ☐ Birth of child _____
- ☐ Break-up, separation, divorce _____
- ☐ Bullying _____
- ☐ Caring for elderly parents _____
- ☐ Changes in physical and or mental health _____
- ☐ Children with school issues and behaviors _____
- ☐ Death _____
- ☐ Disability _____
- ☐ Disappointments _____
- ☐ Discrimination _____
- ☐ Eviction/homelessness _____
- ☐ Family member in the service _____
- ☐ Fighting _____
- ☐ Financial problems or concerns _____
- ☐ Gang-related events _____
- ☐ Harm to self _____
- ☐ Incarceration _____
- ☐ Injury or disability _____
- ☐ Loss of employment _____
- ☐ Medical expenses _____
- ☐ Moodiness _____
- ☐ Moving _____
- ☐ Natural disasters _____
- ☐ Neglect _____
- ☐ Neighbors _____
- ☐ PTSD _____
- ☐ Separation/divorce _____
- ☐ Substance abuse _____
- ☐ Suicide thoughts _____
- ☐ Theft _____
- ☐ Trouble with law _____
- ☐ Unplanned pregnancy _____
- ☐ Verbal, sexual, emotional or physical abuse _____
- ☐ Veteran homecoming _____
- ☐ Workplace/job issues _____
- ☐ Other _____
- ☐ Other _____
- ☐ Other _____
- ☐ Other _____

The Story of Our Change

Telling your story can be enlightening! Often family members want to deny that changes are occurring and disrupting the family dynamics. A great way to tell your story safely is by writing it out or drawing pictures of it. In the space that follows, write or draw in as much detail as possible about the changes and stress that are occurring in your family. Use the back of this page if you need additional space.

Family Changes

In the Midst of Change

One of the best ways for families to deal with the stress of change is to accept the fact that they are in the midst of a change – not to avoid it or deny it.

Describe your current change. _____

_____

_____

_____

_____

_____

_____

Have you been thinking about the change or avoiding it? Explain. _____

_____

_____

_____

_____

How does that work for you? _____

_____

_____

_____

_____

With whom can you talk with about the change? _____

_____

_____

_____

_____

Family Change & Crisis Workbook

Processing the Family Change
(For the adults in the family)

Think about the change your family is currently going through. Journaling about that change and the stress related to the change can help you understand it and reduce your distress. Below, journal about your perception of the change you and/or your family is experiencing.

Describe the change. _____
_____
_____
_____
_____
_____
_____
_____

How does the stress affect certain family members or the entire family? Explain. _____
_____
_____
_____
_____
_____

Did the stress occur gradually or was it without warning? Explain. _____
_____
_____
_____
_____

(Continued on the next page.)

Processing the Family Change *(Continued)*

How are you coping with the stress? _____
_____
_____
_____
_____
_____

How aren't you coping with the stress? _____
_____
_____
_____
_____
_____

Who is helping you to cope with the stress? How? _____
_____
_____
_____
_____
_____

How can you get even more help to manage your stress? _____
_____
_____
_____

Impacting the Stressors of our Change

Think about what roles each of the family members played (including yourself) in the change the family is currently experiencing.

Describe the family change:

_____

_____

Members of the Family and Their Roles in the Stress (including yourself)	How Each Family Member Reacts to the Change	How Each Family Member Can Help Reduce the Stress for Everyone
Example: Dad	takes it out on everyone.	He needs to take a walk outside or talk to mom, and just calm down.

Family Changes

My Worries

During times of change, family members experience a wide variety of worries.
These worries will disrupt a family unit.
What are your worries about the changes your family is experiencing?
In the spaces below, identify your worries and how they affect you, and how your worries affect members of your family.

My Worry	How it Affects Me	How My Worry Affects Our Family as a Whole or Individually

With whom can you talk about your worries?

_____

_____

_____

Logical or Illogical Thoughts?

Change can initiate logical thinking or illogical thinking among family members. Many of the feelings you have about the change your family is facing are related to either logical or illogical thoughts.

In the spaces below, identify the thoughts you are experiencing related to your family change(s) and whether they are **logical** *(true)* or **illogical** *(not thinking about things in a reasonable, sensible way)*.

Your Thoughts about the Changes in Your Family Life	Are they Logical or Illogical?	Explain
Example: I will NEVER be happy being at home.	Illogical	Things change and they can get better. We'll solve our problems and then we won't be so tense.

Would you say that most of your thoughts are logical or illogical?

_____

_____

With whom can you talk to help you sort out whether your thoughts are logical or illogical?

_____

_____

Family Changes

ME - Before & After the Change

The way you think about yourself often changes as a result of stressful times. In the spaces below, write about or list words and phrases that describe the way you were before the change(s) and then after the change(s).

ME – Before the Change(s)	ME – After the Change(s)

What are the positive differences?

_____

_____

What are the negative differences?

_____

_____

US - Before & After the Change

The way you think about your family and family life changes as a result of stressful times.
In the spaces below write about or list words and phrases that describe the way your family, and your family life, were before the change(s) and then after the change(s).

MY FAMILY – Before the Change(s)	MY FAMILY – After the Change(s)

What are the positive differences?

_____

_____

What are the negative differences?

_____

_____

Family Changes

What Do I Look Like?

Think about what you look like when you're **STRESSED**, ○········> and then what you look like when you're *calm!*

I look like this when I am **STRESSED** out!	I look like this when I am calm!

⋯⋯ When are you like this? ↑ ⋯⋯ When are you like this? ↑

_____   _____

_____   _____

_____   _____

CHAPTER II

Family Crisis

For the Facilitator

Explanation of the four scales in this chapter

As the facilitator, you may choose any combination of assessments that will work for each of the particular families with whom you are working.

You may choose to use one scale or all of them,
depending on the make-up of the family and the number of people in the family.

Photocopy as many of each as needed.

1. **One for each child/teen** to identity personal feelings

2. **One for each child/teen** to identify perceptions of adults' feelings

3. **One for each adult** to identity personal feelings

4. **One for each adult** to identify perceptions of children's or teens' feelings

**You will need to photocopy the corresponding
Introduction and Directions
for each scale you administer.**

Chapter II – *Family Crisis* Skills

These skills are behavioral objectives which family members will meet
as they engage in the assessments and guided self-exploration activities.

Children/Teens
Identify their own thoughts, feelings and behaviors related to their family's crises and their perceptions of one or more adults' thoughts, feelings and behaviors in the family setting by responding to five prompts in each of these categories:
　　Denial
　　Heightened Tension
　　Processing Emotions
　　Resolution

Adults
Identify their own thoughts, feelings and behaviors related to their family's crises and their perceptions of one or more children/teens' thoughts, feelings and behaviors in the family setting by responding to five prompts in the above listed categories.

All Family Members

- Assess *Family Crisis* scores as low, moderate or high on the *Scale Profile Interpretation*.
- Identify their scores' meanings based on the *Scale Profile Interpretation* and *Scale Descriptions*.
- Compare their perceptions by entering scores onto a *Family Crisis Scale*.
- Process a crisis situation

    denial and silence

    heightened tension

    emotions and thinking

    resolution.
- Specify avoided issues, what to discuss, how to begin, and benefits of the conversations.
- Identify members one withdraws from, reasons, what can be done, and with whom to discuss this.
- State four problems that are trivialized or blown out of proportion, and ways to avoid

    the reactions.
- Document a tense conversation, and what could have been said differently to reduce stress.
- Identify whom one criticizes, reasons, responses, and what can be done to reduce criticism.
- Describe six situations that trigger negative and positive emotions, and the members involved.
- Communicate using: "When you …, I feel …, I would prefer that you …" to reduce anger.
- Identify four ways one is stuck in negativity, reasons, and with whom to talk about feelings.
- Discuss seven aspects of guilt about a family crisis.
- Journal about negative and positive emotions related to a family crisis.

Family Crisis Scale
Introduction & Directions

By exploring how you and your family members are dealing with stress because of the changes in your family's structure and conditions, you can better work your way through the process for resolving family crises.

This scale explores how you and your family are coping with your crises.
Read each of the statements and decide whether or not the statement describes you.
This assessment contains 20 statements. Read each of the statements and decide how descriptive each statement is of you. In each of the choices listed, circle the number of your response on the line to the right of each statement.

Examples

Scale # 1 and # 3 (Individual's responses)

In the following example, the circled number 2 under "TRUE" indicates the statement is descriptive of the person completing the scale.

Regarding our family crises, which is _____.

	TRUE	FALSE
I usually deny that there is a problem	(2)	1

Scale # 2 and # 4: (Individual's perceptions)

In the following example, the circled number 1 under "FALSE" indicates the person who is completing the scale believes that this statement is not descriptive of the other family member.

Regarding our family crises, which is _____. I believe that this adult ...

	TRUE	FALSE
usually denies that there is a problem	2	(1)

This is not a test. Since there are no right or wrong answers, do not spend too much time thinking about your answers. Be sure to respond to every statement.

(Turn to the next page and begin.)

Family Change & Crisis Workbook

SCALE #1
Child's/Teen's *Family Crisis*

Child's/Teen's Name _____ Date _____

Regarding our family crises, which is _____.

	TRUE	FALSE
I usually deny that there is a problem	2	1
I don't have a problem with it	2	1
If I don't acknowledge it, it'll go away	2	1
It's best not to talk about it	2	1
I don't believe it is that bad	2	1

A TOTAL = _____

	TRUE	FALSE
I am tense about the situation	2	1
I get into more arguments or fights lately	2	1
I am snapping at other family members	2	1
I am experiencing conflicts	2	1
I don't seem to trust others	2	1

B TOTAL = _____

	TRUE	FALSE
I really don't show my emotions	2	1
I don't know how to express my emotions	2	1
I feel helpless about the situation	2	1
My emotions get the best of me and I can't control them	2	1
Small things trigger my negative emotions	2	1

C TOTAL = _____

	TRUE	FALSE
I am not working to resolve my problems within the family	2	1
I am not coping well with my issues	2	1
I am feeling like giving up	2	1
I have identified all the things wrong with my family	2	1
I have not learned how to manage this crisis	2	1

D TOTAL = _____

SCALE #1
Child's/Teen's *Family Crisis*
Scale Scoring Directions

Child's/Teen's Name _____ Date _____

This scale is designed to measure how effectively you and your family are in coping and managing your current crisis.

For the sections you just completed, add the numbers that you circled.
You will have a total in the range from 5 to 10 for each one. Transfer these totals to the spaces below.
Then add your four scores to get your GRAND TOTAL.

        A   Denial   Total = _____
        B   Heightened Tension   Total = _____
        C   Processing Emotions   Total = _____
        D   Resolution   Total = _____
                              GRAND Total = _____

Scale Profile Interpretation

Individual Score	Grand Total	Result	Indications
5 - 6	20 - 26	Low	Low scores indicate that you are not being too affected by your family crisis.
7 - 8	27 - 33	Moderate	Moderate scores indicate that you are being somewhat affected by your family issues or crisis.
9 - 10	34 - 40	High	High scores indicate that you are being extremely affected by your family issues or crisis.

Individual Scale Descriptions

Denial – The child or teen scoring high on this scale tends to be in denial that a problem exists regarding the family's issues.
Heightened Tension – The child or teen scoring high on this scale tends to believe that the stress and tension that exists are becoming greater regarding the family's issues.
Processing Emotions – The child or teen scoring high on this scale tends to have difficulty coping with emotions regarding the family's crisis.
Resolution – The child or teen scoring high on this scale is struggling to decide how to begin to resolve the family's crisis.
GRAND TOTAL – The child or teen scoring high on the total of all the scores is having a difficult time and is being highly affected by the family's crisis.

Family Change & Crisis Workbook

SCALE #2
Child's/Teen's Perception of an Adult's *Family Crisis*

Child's/Teen's Name _____

Adult's Name _____ Date _____

Regarding this family crisis, _____. I believe that this adult …

	TRUE	FALSE
usually denies that there is a problem	2	1
doesn't have a problem with it	2	1
does not acknowledge it, thinking it'll go away	2	1
thinks it's best not to talk about it	2	1
doesn't believe it is that bad	2	1

A TOTAL = _____

	TRUE	FALSE
is tense about the situation	2	1
gets into more arguments or fights lately	2	1
is snapping at other family members	2	1
experiences conflicts	2	1
doesn't seem to trust certain others	2	1

B TOTAL = _____

	TRUE	FALSE
doesn't show emotions	2	1
doesn't know how to express feelings	2	1
feels helpless about the situation	2	1
can't control emotions	2	1
allows small things to trigger negative emotions	2	1

C TOTAL = _____

	TRUE	FALSE
is not working to resolve problems within the family	2	1
is not coping well with issues	2	1
feels like giving up	2	1
has identified all the things wrong with the family	2	1
has not learned how to manage this crisis	2	1

D TOTAL = _____

Family Crisis

SCALE #2
Child's/Teen's Perception of an Adult's *Family Crisis* Scale Scoring Directions

Child's/Teen's Name _____

Adult's Name _____ Date _____

This scale is designed to measure how effectively you perceive the above adult is coping and managing your family's crisis.

For the sections you just completed, add the numbers that you circled.
You will have a total in the range from 5 to 10 for each one. Transfer these totals to the spaces below.
Then add your four scores to get your GRAND TOTAL

A	Denial	Total =	_____
B	Heightened Tension	Total =	_____
C	Processing Emotions	Total =	_____
D	Resolution	Total =	_____
		GRAND Total =	_____

Scale Profile Interpretation

Individual Score	Grand Total	Result	Indications
5 - 6	20 - 26	Low	Low scores indicate that you perceive the above named adult is not being too affected by your family issues or crisis.
7 - 8	27 - 33	Moderate	Moderate scores indicate that you perceive the above named adult is being somewhat affected by your family issues or crisis.
9 - 10	34 - 40	High	High scores indicate that you perceive the above named adult is being extremely affected by your family issues or crisis.

Individual Scale Descriptions

Denial – The child or teen scoring high on this scale perceives that the above stated adult tends to be in denial that a problem exists regarding the family's crisis.

Heightened Tension – The child or teen scoring high on this scale perceives that the above stated adult tends to believe that the stress and tension that exists is getting greater regarding the family's crisis.

Processing Emotions – The child or teen scoring high on this scale perceives that the above stated adult tends to have difficulty coping with emotions regarding the family's crisis.

Resolution – The child or teen scoring high on this scale perceives that the above stated adult is struggling with how to begin to resolve the family's crisis.

GRAND TOTAL – The child or teen scoring high on the total of all the scores perceives that the above stated adult is having a difficult time and is being highly affected by the family's crisis.

Family Change & Crisis Workbook

SCALE #3
Adult's *Family Crisis*

Adult's Name _____ Date _____

Regarding this family crises, _____.

	TRUE	FALSE
I usually deny that there is a problem	2	1
I don't have a problem with it	2	1
If I don't acknowledge it, it'll go away	2	1
It's best not to talk about it	2	1
I don't believe it is that bad	2	1

A TOTAL = _____

	TRUE	FALSE
I am tense about the situation	2	1
I get into more arguments or fights lately	2	1
I am snapping at other family members	2	1
I am experiencing conflicts	2	1
I don't seem to trust others	2	1

B TOTAL = _____

	TRUE	FALSE
I really don't show my emotions	2	1
I don't know how to express my emotions	2	1
I feel helpless about the situation	2	1
My emotions get the best of me and I can't control them	2	1
Small things trigger my negative emotions	2	1

C TOTAL = _____

	TRUE	FALSE
I am not working to resolve my problems within the family	2	1
I am not coping well with my issues	2	1
I am feeling like giving up	2	1
I have identified all the things wrong with my family	2	1
I have not learned how to manage this crisis	2	1

D TOTAL = _____

SCALE #3
Adult's *Family Crisis*
Scale Scoring Directions

Adult's Name _____ Date _____

This scale is designed to measure how effectively you and your family are in coping and managing your current crisis.

For the sections you just completed, add the numbers that you circled.
You will have a total in the range from 5 to 10 for each one. Transfer these totals to the spaces below.
Then add your four scores to get your GRAND TOTAL.

        A   Denial   Total = _____
        B   Heightened Tension   Total = _____
        C   Processing Emotions   Total = _____
        D   Resolution   Total = _____
                                                  GRAND Total = _____

Scale Profile Interpretation

Individual Score	Grand Total	Result	Indications
5 - 6	20 - 26	Low	Low scores indicate that you are not being too affected by your family crisis.
7 - 8	27 - 33	Moderate	Moderate scores indicate that you are being somewhat affected by your family issues or crisis.
9 - 10	34 - 40	High	High scores indicate that you are being extremely affected by your family issues or crisis.

Individual Scale Descriptions

Denial – The adult scoring high on this scale tends to be in denial that a problem exists regarding the family's crisis or issues.
Heightened Tension – The adult scoring high on this scale tends to believe that the stress and tension that exists is getting greater regarding the family's crisis or issues.
Processing Emotions – The adult scoring high on this scale tends to have difficulty coping with emotions regarding the family's crisis or issues.
Resolution – The adult scoring high on this scale is struggling with how to begin to resolve the family's crisis or issues.
GRAND TOTAL – The child or teen scoring high on the total of all the scores is having a difficult time and is being highly affected by the family's crisis or issues.

Family Change & Crisis Workbook

SCALE #4
Adult's Perception of a Child's/Teen's *Family Crisis*

Adult's Name _____

Child's/Teen's Name _____ Date _____

Regarding this family crisis, _____. I believe that this child or teen …

	TRUE	FALSE
usually denies that there is a problem	2	1
doesn't have a problem with it	2	1
does not acknowledge it, thinking it'll go away	2	1
thinks it's best not to talk about it	2	1
doesn't believe it is that bad	2	1

A TOTAL = _____

	TRUE	FALSE
is tense about the situation	2	1
gets into more arguments or fights lately	2	1
is snapping at other family members	2	1
experiences conflicts	2	1
doesn't seem to trust certain others	2	1

B TOTAL = _____

	TRUE	FALSE
doesn't show emotions	2	1
doesn't know how to express feelings	2	1
feels helpless about the situation	2	1
can't control emotions	2	1
allows small things to trigger negative emotions	2	1

C TOTAL = _____

	TRUE	FALSE
is not working to resolve problems within the family	2	1
is not coping well with issues	2	1
feels like giving up	2	1
has identified all the things wrong with the family	2	1
has not learned how to manage this crisis	2	1

D TOTAL = _____

Family Crisis

SCALE #4
Adult's Perception of a Child's/Teen's *Family Crisis*
Scale Scoring Directions

Adult's Name _____

Child's/Teen's Name _____ Date _____

This scale is designed to measure how effectively you perceive the above child or teen is coping and managing your family's crisis.
For the sections you just completed, add the numbers that you circled.
You will have a total in the range from 5 to 10 for each one. Transfer these totals to the spaces below.
Then add your four scores to get your GRAND TOTAL

    A   **Denial**   Total = _____
    B   **Heightened Tension**   Total = _____
    C   **Processing Emotions**   Total = _____
    D   **Resolution**   Total = _____
                       GRAND Total = _____

Scale Profile Interpretation

Individual Score	Grand Total	Result	Indications
5 - 6	20 - 26	Low	Low scores indicate that you perceive the above named child or teen is not being too affected by your family issues or crisis.
7 - 8	27 - 33	Moderate	Moderate scores indicate that you perceive the above named child or teen is being somewhat affected by your family issues or crisis.
9 - 10	34 - 40	High	High scores indicate that you perceive the above named child or teen is being extremely affected by your family issues or crisis.

Individual Scale Descriptions

Denial – The adult scoring high on this scale perceives that the above stated child or teen tends to be in denial that a problem exists regarding the family's crisis.
Heightened Tension – The adult scoring high on this scale perceives that the above stated child or teen tends to believe that the stress and tension that exists is getting greater regarding the family's crisis.
Processing Emotions – The adult scoring high on this scale perceives that the above stated child or teen tends to have difficulty coping with emotions regarding the family's crises.
Resolution – The adult scoring high on this scale perceives that the above stated child or teen is struggling with how to begin to resolve the family's crisis.
GRAND TOTAL – The adult scoring high on the total of all the scores perceives that the above stated child or teen is having a difficult time, and is being highly affected by the family's crisis.

Family Crisis Scale
Family Score Totals

For each of the items on the scales, insert the person's name completing the scale, and transfer each person's scale on one line below.

Scale 1 Name (Child's/Teen's Scale)	Score Denial	Score Heightened Tension	Score Processing Emotions	Score Resolution	TOTAL SCORE
(example) John	10	6	8	5	29

Scale 2 Name (Child's/Teen's Perception of Adult Scale)	Score Denial	Score Heightened Tension	Score Processing Emotions	Score Resolution	TOTAL SCORE

Scale 3 Name (Adult's Identity Scale)	Score Denial	Score Heightened Tension	Score Processing Emotions	Score Resolution	TOTAL SCORE

Scale 4 Name (Adult's Perception of Child's/Teen's Scale)	Score Denial	Score Heightened Tension	Score Processing Emotions	Score Resolution	TOTAL SCORE

Family Crisis

Processing a Crisis Situation

Like individuals, families also face challenging situations due to a change.
This change brings on stress that can lead to a family crisis.
When you go through crisis as a family, you experience a variety of feelings:

DENIAL AND SILENCE
At first, people have the belief that the problem isn't that bad. They feel as if this could never happen to them, but it has! At this point, it is time to acknowledge the situation and begin to deal with it. Family members at this point are possibly trying to keep the problem at a minimum and are not communicating their feelings to one another. In reality, it is best to face the situation, talk about it, and begin to deal with it.

The biggest crisis situation is _____

_____

_____

_____

Are you ignoring and denying this crisis by not facing up to it? How? _____

_____

_____

_____

_____

Describe what you see as the reality of the situation right now. _____

_____

_____

_____

_____

Who in your family can you talk with about this situation? _____

_____

_____

_____

_____

Who else is a trusted person you can talk with? _____

_____

_____

_____

_____

(Continued on the next page.)

Processing a Crisis Situation (Continued)

HEIGHTENED TENSION
Increased tension in a family comes about in the form of silence, fights, arguments, and/or conflicts.

What is one of your intense situations in your family? _____
_____
_____
_____
_____

Who are the other people involved in this tense situation? _____
_____
_____
_____
_____

Why do you think you and these other people are fighting, arguing, disagreeing and/or not talking at all?
_____
_____
_____
_____
_____
_____
_____
_____
_____

With whom in your family can you talk about how to resolve this intense this situation? _____
_____
_____
_____

Who else is a trusted person you can talk with?_____
_____
_____
_____
_____

(Continued on the next page.)

Family Crisis

Processing a Crisis Situation *(Continued)*

EMOTIONS & THINKING
When family members feel helpless, angry, sad, etc., they need support, and it is important for them to be able to explain the situation to someone whom they trust and with whom they feel comfortable.

Explain how you are feeling about the crisis situation at the present time. _____
_____
_____
_____
_____

In what ways does the situation seem hopeless _____
_____
_____
_____
_____

In what ways does the situation feel hopeful? _____
_____
_____
_____
_____

What kind of support do you need? _____
_____
_____
_____
_____

Who is a trusted person who can give you that support? _____
_____
_____
_____
_____
_____

(Continued on the next page.)

Processing a Crisis Situation *(Continued)*

RESOLUTION

When family members support each other, this support often brings some type of a resolution or plan to resolve the situation. Specific steps can be taken to make the best of the situation, to detail a plan for resolving the situation, and develop ways for the family to accommodate to a new situation.

Have you had a situation that needed to be resolved in your family? _____
_____
_____

Explain the situation. _____
_____
_____
_____
_____

How was it resolved? _____
_____
_____
_____
_____

What did you learn from it? _____
_____
_____
_____
_____

If it was not resolved, what is your next step in trying to get it resolved? _____
_____
_____
_____

Who can support you in resolving the situation? _____
_____
_____
_____

Family Crisis

Let's Discuss It!

Many people avoid discussing their problems, and this leads to additional stress and typically a crisis. Talking things out and working towards finding a solution is always the best way to reduce the stress and emotions that make family problems worse.

People with Whom I Am Avoiding a Discussion and Why	We Need to Discuss …	Benefits of this Conversation Would be …
EXAMPLE: My step-sister, Sue. She is angry at me for coming into her life.	Her attitude toward my sharing her room.	We could have fun, decorate it together, and accept that it's okay to share.
1.		
2.		
3.		
4.		

How can you begin these discussions?

1. _____

_____

_____

2. _____

_____

_____

3. _____

_____

_____

4. _____

_____

_____

Family Change & Crisis Workbook

Withdrawing

During times of stress, many family members feel like withdrawing from each other, which tends to create an even tenser atmosphere.

Below, explore your family relationships. From whom are you withdrawing?

Family Members from Whom I Withdraw	Why I Withdraw	What Can I Do About It?

Are there family members whom you want to continue to withdraw from? _____

Why? _____

_____

With whom can you discuss this? _____

_____

Family Crisis

Problems

All problems have associated stress. Many family members tend to trivialize family problems, or blow them out of proportion, thus blurring the impact on the family unit. There is no such thing as a little problem. If it's a problem, it needs to be dealt with in non-threatening and non-blaming approaches. Any problem, regardless of how big or small, is a stressor for the individual and can ultimately cause stress for the family.

Below, identify some of the problems that you have encountered with the people in your family.

The Problem and with Whom?	Do you trivialize it or blow it out of proportion? How?	Does the other person trivialize it or blow it out of proportion? How?
1.		
2.		
3.		
4.		

How can you begin discussions with these people to try to avoid the different reactions?

1. _____
_____

2. _____
_____

3. _____
_____

4. _____
_____

Family Change & Crisis Workbook

Tension

Tension in a household is often the result of stress due to a family crisis. Facing the same issue, tension can be noticed among many members or just one, or only a few. Below, identify one situation's conversation in which you were involved, which caused you to become tense. (See example below.)

Example: I or Dad said <u>"You went out with Jane last night!"</u> *The response from me was <u>"Yes, we went to the movies!"</u>*
Then this was said. <u>Dad said "I told you I don't like her."</u> *And the response was <u>"I'm 18 and can make my own decisions"</u>*

I or _____ said… **The response from _____ was …**

Then this was said … **And the response was …**

What could have been said differently on your part that would have made the situation less tense? _____
_____
_____

What could have been said differently on the other person's part? _____
_____
_____

Family Crisis

Ways I'm Critical

Being constantly overly critical of other members of your family will not help you, or the problem. Criticism is about the person, not about the task.
(What is wrong with you? opposed to I need you to do what you're supposed to do.)
In fact, it will create more stress.

In the table that follows, identify how and with whom you tend to be overly critical.

Family Members I Often Criticize	Of What I am Usually Critical	How This Upsets Others
EXAMPLE: My little brother Joe, who is unreliable.	He doesn't always wipe the dishes when it's his turn. Then I need to. I get very angry at him and tell him he never does anything he is supposed to (even though he usually does)! We do a lot of yelling. He cries.	Mom gets upset with me because I'm older and "should know better". She yells at my brother. He's mad at me. Then Mom's angry the rest of the night. Everyone else is unhappy because Mom's angry.

Which of these people do you criticize most often, and why? _____
_____
_____

What can you do about it? _____
_____
_____

Negative and Positive Emotions

To more rapidly process the crisis your family is experiencing, it is important for you to understand your feelings and be aware of what triggers them. The first step is to identify the situations that trigger your emotions. It is important to recognize that feelings don't just happen.

As you are thinking about the crisis in your family, identify those family situations that trigger your negative emotions. *(Example: Someone enters my room without knocking.)*

Situations Related to the Crisis that Triggers *Negative* Emotions for Me	Family Members Involved	Emotions I Experience

Next, as you are thinking about the crisis in your family, identify those family situations that trigger your positive emotions. *(Example: Getting a hug for "no reason at all.")*

Situations Related to the Crisis that Triggers *Positive* Emotions for Me	Family Members Involved	Emotions I Experience

Family Crisis

Expressing How You Feel

It is important for family members to be able to express their emotions effectively. The following is an excellent way to ensure that you are communicating your feelings in an open, honest, direct and accepting way.

EXAMPLE:
What is something that a member of your family does or says that upsets or angers you?
How do you typically react in this situation?
Communicate more effectively by saying …
   "When you grounded me for a month because I was 15 minutes late coming home I felt you were giving me an unreasonable punishment. I would have preferred that you had considered that it was the first time I was ever late coming home."

Now you try it with a situation that has happened with you and a member of your family.

Step 1: What is something that a member of your family does or says that upsets or angers you?

_____
_____
_____
_____

Step 2: Explore how you typically react.

_____
_____
_____
_____

Step 3: Communicate more effectively by saying …

When you _____

_____

I feel _____

I would prefer that you _____

_____
_____
_____

Stuck in Negative Feelings?

When experiencing a crisis in the family, especially when there has been a major change or many changes at the same time, it is easy for family members to get stuck in negative feelings and have difficulty in overcoming them.

I have no interest in these family activities _____

_____

_____

because _____

_____

I feel differently than I did in the past about family members _____

_____

_____

because _____

_____

I don't want to interact with the following family members _____

_____

_____

because _____

_____

I feel sad a lot of the time _____

_____

_____

because _____

_____

I can talk to _____

_____

_____

_____

_____ about being stuck!

Guilt about the Family Crisis

Think about the change that is leading to a crisis in your family. Often people have guilt about what the family is experiencing! Journal about it below.

State the change:

How do you feel about the change?

How were things before the change?

What part did you play in the eventual change?

What did or didn't you do that may have played a part in the eventual change?

Do you feel you could have done something differently? Explain.

Did you do what you did with the best of intentions?

With whom can you talk about these feelings?

Dear Journal

People going through a crisis need to allow themselves to experience what they are feeling by expressing it. Journaling provides a perfect method for silently doing so.

Write about one crisis you are experiencing in your home arrangement or in your family. Enter both positive and negative emotions.

CHAPTER III

Family Stress

For the Facilitator

Explanation of the four scales in this chapter

As the facilitator, you may choose any combination of assessments that will work for each of the particular families with whom you are working.

You may choose to use one scale or all of them,
depending on the make-up of the family and the number of people in the family.

Photocopy as many of each as needed.

1. **One for each child/teen** to identity personal feelings

2. **One for each child/teen** to identify perceptions of adults' feelings

3. **One for each adult** to identity personal feelings

4. **One for each adult** to identify perceptions of children's or teens' feelings

**You will need to photocopy the corresponding
Introduction and Directions
for each scale you administer.**

Chapter III – *Family Stress* Skills

These skills are behavioral objectives which family members will meet as they engage in the assessments and guided self-exploration activities.

Children/Teens
Identify their own thoughts, feelings and behaviors related to their family's stress and their perceptions of one or more adults' thoughts, feelings and behaviors in the family setting by responding to six prompts in each of these categories:
   Avoiding Blame
   Communication
   Managing Emotions
   Problem Solving.

Adults
Identify their own thoughts, feelings and behaviors related to their family's stress and their perceptions of one or more children/teens' thoughts, feelings and behaviors in the family setting by responding to five prompts in the above listed categories.

All Family Members
- Assess *Family Stress* scores as low, moderate or high on the *Scale Profile Interpretation*.
- Identify scores' meanings based on the *Scale Profile Interpretation* and *Individual Scale Descriptions*.
- Compare their perceptions by entering scores onto a *Family Stress Scale*.
- Identify nine unhealthy ways to manage stress, how they seem to help, and ways to overcome them.
- Identify types of lies, family members who may lie, reasons, effects, and ways to regain trust.
- Name five members to forgive, reasons, and benefits to self, the person, and the family.
- Process the difficulty of forgiving, and the value of not forgetting lessons learned.
- Write a script incorporating five tips for fair fighting; note the expected responses.
- Focus on positive aspects and family fun by completing six sentences.
- Specify eight or more stress management strategies used individually, and/or with the family.
- Identify support systems within and outside the family.
- Summarize acceptance of the change, feelings, effects, and the resultant opportunities.
- Differentiate between factors that are or are not under personal control.
- Describe four fears, whether each is realistic, what can be done, and with whom to talk.
- Name family members, their positive qualities, and ways to convey appreciation.
- Identify people one blames for the change, reasons, and their sides of the story.
- Reframe the change: note what was learned, a positive outcome, and a possible opportunity.
- State six aspects of coping with change in routines, and how to incorporate positive habits.
- Document details for each of four steps in a family problem solving system.

Family Stress

Child's/Teen's – *Family Stress Scale*
Introduction & Directions

Family stress is an outgrowth of changes, or perspective changes, in the family unit. These changes can be positive changes *(adult family member being promoted to another city)* or negative *(adult family member losing job)*. The changes can also be either negative or positive for different family members *(adult being promoted to a great new job in a different city, teen needing to change schools and make new friends.)* Regardless of the type of stress, family members must learn how to effectively manage the stress.

The *Family Stress* Scale can help you explore how well you are managing the stressors in your life right now, as well as how you feel the others are handling it. This scale contains 24 statements. Read each of the statements and decide how descriptive the statement is of you or your family member. In each of the choices listed, circle the number of your response on the line to the right of each statement.

Examples

Scale # 1 and # 3 (Individual's responses)

In the following example, the circled number 1 under "Rarely/Never" indicates the statement is rarely or never true **of the person completing the scale**.

Regarding our family stressors ...

	ALWAYS	SOMETIMES	RARELY/NEVER
I believe that certain family members are to blame	3	2	①

Scale # 2 and # 4: (Individual's perceptions)

In the following example, the circled number 3 under "Always" indicates the person who is completing the scale perceives that this statement is always true **about the other family member**.

Regarding our family stressors, I believe that this adult ...

	ALWAYS	SOMETIMES	RARELY/NEVER
I believe that certain family members are to blame	③	2	1

This is not a test and there are no right or wrong answers. Do not spend too much time thinking about your answers. Your initial response will be the most true for you. Be sure to respond to every statement.

(Turn to the next page and begin.)

Family Change & Crisis Workbook

SCALE #1
Child's/Teen's *Family Stress*

Child's/Teen's Name _____ Date _____

Regarding our family stressors ...

	ALWAYS	SOMETIMES	RARELY/NEVER
I believe that certain family members are to blame	3	2	1
I lie to other family members	3	2	1
I look for ways to avoid blame	3	2	1
I am critical in discussing behaviors	3	2	1
I get defensive when discussing the change	3	2	1
I look for a scapegoat	3	2	1

A TOTAL = _____

	ALWAYS	SOMETIMES	RARELY/NEVER
I do not communicate openly	3	2	1
I do express my honest feelings	3	2	1
I keep secrets from other family members	3	2	1
I am afraid to discuss the matter	3	2	1
I talk around the subject, but not about it directly	3	2	1
I feel like I cannot talk to certain family members	3	2	1

C TOTAL = _____

	ALWAYS	SOMETIMES	RARELY/NEVER
I easily become emotionally overwhelmed	3	2	1
I let my emotions control me	3	2	1
I overreact to what family members say	3	2	1
I do not know what causes some of my emotions	3	2	1
I see things as worse than they really are	3	2	1
I always say "you should of ..." to myself	3	2	1

M TOTAL = _____

	ALWAYS	SOMETIMES	RARELY/NEVER
I believe I will have a hard time solving the problem	3	2	1
I believe my family will not always stick together	3	2	1
I believe we cannot handle stress as a family	3	2	1
I believe I have no control over my future	3	2	1
I try not to think about and avoid my problems	3	2	1
I don't trust other members enough to solve my issues	3	2	1

P TOTAL = _____

Family Stress

SCALE #1
Child's/Teen's *Family Stress*
Scale Scoring Directions

Child's/Teen's Name _____ Date _____

All family members encounter stress. The healthier the family member and the family unit as a whole, the more resilient they are and able to manage their stress well.

Add the numbers you circled on the scale and write that score on the line marked TOTAL.

Then transfer that total to the space below.

After you transfer your scores, add them to get your GRAND TOTAL:

A	Avoiding Blame	Total = _____
C	Communication	Total = _____
M	Managing Emotions	Total = _____
P	Probem Solving	Total = _____
		GRAND Total = _____

Scale Profile Interpretation

Individual Score	Grand Total	Result	Indications
6 - 9	24 - 39	Low	Low Scores indicate that you have developed many of the necessary coping skills for managing your family stress.
10 - 14	40 - 56	Moderate	Moderate Scores indicate that you have developed some of the necessary coping skills for managing your family stress.
15 - 18	57 - 72	High	High Scores indicate that you have not developed the necessary coping skills for managing your family stress.

Individual Scale Descriptions

Avoiding Blame – The child/teen scoring High on this scale blames other family members for family stress, does everything to deflect any blame for the situation to other family members, and looks for a scapegoat for the situation.

Communication – The child/teen scoring High on this scale does not communicate openly and honestly, does not trust confiding in some other family members, and will keep secrets.

Managing Emotions – The child/teen scoring High on this scale allows emotions to be in control in life, often overreacts and then gets overwhelmed by emotions, and is often unaware of the situations that trigger emotional outbreaks.

Problem Solving – The child/teen scoring High on this scale does not believe that anyone in the family, has the ability to solve problems they encounter, or that family members will stick together enough to solve problems that cause the family stress.

GRAND TOTAL – The child/teen scoring High on the total of all four scales does not feel that anyone in the family unit as a whole has the coping skills to manage the stress they encounter; they blame each other; they fail to communicate well; they demonstrate unhealthy emotions; and they have trouble solving problems.

Family Change & Crisis Workbook

SCALE #2
Child's/Teen's Perception of an Adult's *Family Stress*

Child's/Teen's Name _____

Adult's Name _____ Date _____

Regarding our family changes, I believe this adult …

	ALWAYS	SOMETIMES	RARELY/NEVER
thinks that certain family members are to blame	3	2	1
lies to me and/or other family members	3	2	1
looks for ways to avoid blame	3	2	1
is critical in discussing behaviors	3	2	1
gets defensive when discussing the change	3	2	1
looks for a scapegoat	3	2	1

A TOTAL = _____

	ALWAYS	SOMETIMES	RARELY/NEVER
does not communicate openly	3	2	1
expresses honest feelings	3	2	1
keeps secrets from other family members	3	2	1
is afraid to discuss the matter	3	2	1
talks around the subject, but not about it directly	3	2	1
feels unable to talk to certain family members	3	2	1

C TOTAL = _____

	ALWAYS	SOMETIMES	RARELY/NEVER
easily becomes emotionally overwhelmed	3	2	1
lets emotions take control	3	2	1
overreacts to what family members say	3	2	1
does not know what causes some emotions	3	2	1
sees things as worse than they really are	3	2	1
says "I should have …" to him or herself	3	2	1

M TOTAL = _____

	ALWAYS	SOMETIMES	RARELY/NEVER
believes we will have a hard time solving the problem	3	2	1
believes our family will not always stick together	3	2	1
believes we do not handle stress as a family	3	2	1
believes no one in the family has control over the future	3	2	1
tries to think avoid problems	3	2	1
doesn't trust other members enough to solve the issues	3	2	1

P TOTAL = _____

Family Stress

SCALE #2
Child's/Teen's Perception of an Adult's *Family Stress* Scale Scoring Directions

Child's/Teen's Name _____

Adult's Name _____ Date _____

All family members encounter stress. The healthier the family member and the family unit as a whole, the more resilient they are and able to manage their stress well.
Add the numbers you circled on the scale and write that score on the line marked TOTAL.
Then transfer that total to the space below.
After you transfer your scores, add them to get your GRAND TOTAL:

- A   Avoiding Blame   Total = _____
- C   Communication   Total = _____
- M   Managing Emotions   Total = _____
- P   Problem Solving   Total = _____
-   GRAND Total = _____

Scale Profile Interpretation

Individual Score	Grand Total	Result	Indications
6 - 9	24 - 39	Low	Low scores indicate that you perceive that the above named adult has developed the coping skills necessary for managing the family stress.
10 - 14	40 - 56	Moderate	Moderate scores indicate that you perceive that the above named adult has developed some of the coping skills necessary for managing the family stress.
15 - 18	57 - 72	High	High scores indicate that you perceive that the above named adult has not developed the coping skills necessary for managing the family stress.

Individual Scale Descriptions

Avoiding Blame – The child/teen scoring High on this scale perceives the above named adult blames other family members for their family stress, does everything to deflect any blame for the situation to other family members and looks for a scapegoat for the situation.

Communication – The child/teen scoring High on this scale perceives the above named adult does not communicate openly and honestly, does not trust confiding in some other family members and keeps secrets.

Managing Emotions – The child/teen scoring High on this scale perceives the above named adult has no control of emotions, often overreacts and then gets overwhelmed by emotions, and is often unaware of the situations that trigger emotional outbreaks.

Problem Solving – The child/teen scoring High on this scale perceives the above named adult does not believe that anyone in the family, has the ability to solve problems they encounter, or will stick together enough to solve problems that cause the family stress.

GRAND TOTAL – The adult scoring high on the total of all the scores perceives that the above stated child or teen is having a difficult time, and is being highly affected by the family's crisis.

SCALE #3
Adult's *Family Stress*

Adult's Name _____ Date _____

Regarding our family changes ...

	ALWAYS	SOMETIMES	RARELY/NEVER
I believe that certain family members are to blame	3	2	1
I lie to other family members	3	2	1
I look for ways to avoid blame	3	2	1
I am critical in discussing behaviors	3	2	1
I get defensive when discussing the change	3	2	1
I look for a scapegoat	3	2	1

A TOTAL = _____

	ALWAYS	SOMETIMES	RARELY/NEVER
I do not communicate openly	3	2	1
I do express my honest feelings	3	2	1
I keep secrets from other family members	3	2	1
I am afraid to discuss the matter	3	2	1
I talk around the subject, but not about it directly	3	2	1
I feel like I cannot talk to certain family members	3	2	1

C TOTAL = _____

	ALWAYS	SOMETIMES	RARELY/NEVER
I easily become emotionally overwhelmed	3	2	1
I let my emotions control me	3	2	1
I overreact to what family members say	3	2	1
I do not know what causes some of my emotions	3	2	1
I see things as worse than they really are	3	2	1
I always say "you should have ..." to myself	3	2	1

M TOTAL = _____

	ALWAYS	SOMETIMES	RARELY/NEVER
I believe I will have a hard time solving the problem	3	2	1
I believe my family will not always stick together	3	2	1
I believe we cannot handle stress as a family	3	2	1
I believe I have no control over my future	3	2	1
I try to avoid my problems	3	2	1
I don't trust other members enough to solve my issues	3	2	1

P TOTAL = _____

SCALE #3
Adult's *Family Stress*
Scale Scoring Directions

Adult's Name _____ Date _____

All family members encounter stress. The healthier the family member and the family unit as a whole, the more resilient they are and able to manage their stress well.

Add the numbers you circled on the scale and write that score on the line marked TOTAL.

Then transfer that total to the space below.

After you transfer your scores, add them to get your GRAND TOTAL:

A	Avoiding Blame	Total = _____
C	Communication	Total = _____
M	Managing Emotions	Total = _____
P	Problem Solving	Total = _____
		GRAND Total = _____

Scale Profile Interpretation

Individual Score	Grand Total	Result	Indications
6 - 9	24 - 39	Low	Low scores indicate that you have developed the coping skills necessary for managing your family stress
10 - 14	40 - 56	Moderate	Moderate scores indicate that you have developed some of the coping skills necessary for managing your family stress.
15 - 18	57 - 72	High	High scores indicate that you have not developed the coping skills necessary for managing your family stress.

Individual Scale Descriptions

Avoiding Blame – The adult scoring High on this scale blames other family members for their family stress, does everything to deflect any blame for the situation to other family members, and looks for a scapegoat for the situation.

Communication – The adult scoring High on this scale does not communicate openly and honestly, does not trust confiding in some other family members, and will keep secrets.

Managing Emotions – The adult scoring High on this scale allows emotions to be in control in life, often overreacts and then gets overwhelmed by emotions, and is often unaware of the situations that trigger emotional outbreaks.

Problem Solving – The adult scoring High on this scale does not believe that anyone in the family, has the ability to solve problems they encounter, or that family members will stick together enough to solve problems that cause the family stress.

GRAND TOTAL – The adult scoring High on the total of all four scales does not feel that anyone in the family unit as a whole has the coping skills to manage the stress they encounter; they blame each other; they fail to communicate well; they demonstrate unhealthy emotions; and they have trouble solving problems.

Family Change & Crisis Workbook

SCALE #4
Adult's Perception of a Child's/Teen's *Family Stress*

Adult's Name _____

Child's/Teen's Name _____ Date _____

Regarding our family changes, I believe this child or teen ...

	ALWAYS	SOMETIMES	RARELY/NEVER
thinks that certain family members are to blame	3	2	1
lies to me and/or other family members	3	2	1
looks for ways to avoid blame	3	2	1
is critical in discussing behaviors	3	2	1
gets defensive when discussing the change	3	2	1
looks for a scapegoat	3	2	1

A TOTAL = _____

	ALWAYS	SOMETIMES	RARELY/NEVER
does not communicate openly	3	2	1
expresses honest feelings	3	2	1
keeps secrets from other family members	3	2	1
is afraid to discuss the matter	3	2	1
talks around the subject, but not about it directly	3	2	1
feels unable to talk to certain family members	3	2	1

C TOTAL = _____

	ALWAYS	SOMETIMES	RARELY/NEVER
easily becomes emotionally overwhelmed	3	2	1
lets emotions take control	3	2	1
overreacts to what family members say	3	2	1
does not know what causes some emotions	3	2	1
sees things as worse than they really are	3	2	1
says "I should have ..." to him or herself	3	2	1

M TOTAL = _____

	ALWAYS	SOMETIMES	RARELY/NEVER
believes we will have a hard time solving the problem	3	2	1
believes our family will not always stick together	3	2	1
believes we do not handle stress as a family	3	2	1
believes no one in the family has control over the future	3	2	1
tries to think avoid problems	3	2	1
doesn't trust other members enough to solve the issues	3	2	1

P TOTAL = _____

Family Stress

SCALE #4
Adult's Perception of a Child's/Teen's *Family Stress* Scale Scoring Directions

Adult's Name _____

Child"s/Teen's Name _____ Date _____

All family members encounter stress. The healthier the family member and the family unit as a whole, the more resilient they are and able to manage their stress well.

Add the numbers you circled on the scale and write that score on the line marked TOTAL.

Then transfer that total to the space below.

After you transfer your scores, add them to get your GRAND TOTAL:

A	Avoiding Blame	Total = _____
C	Communication	Total = _____
M	Managing Emotions	Total = _____
P	Problem Solving	Total = _____
		GRAND Total = _____

Scale Profile Interpretation

Individual Score	Grand Total	Result	Indications
6 - 9	24 - 39	Low	Low scores indicate that you perceive that the above named child or teen has developed the coping skills necessary for managing the family stress.
10 - 14	40 - 56	Moderate	Moderate scores indicate that you perceive that the above named child or teen has developed some of the coping skills necessary for managing the family stress.
15 - 18	57 - 72	High	High scores indicate that you perceive that the above named child or teen has have not developed the coping skills necessary for managing the family stress.

Individual Scale Descriptions

Avoiding Blame – The adult scoring High on this scale perceives the above named child or teen blames other family members for their family stress, does everything to deflect any blame for the situation to other family members and looks for a scapegoat for the situation.

Communication – The adult scoring High on this scale perceives the above named child or teen does not communicate openly and honestly, does not trust confiding in some other family members and keeps secrets.

Managing Emotions – The adult scoring High on this scale perceives the above named child or teen has not control of emotions, often overreacts and then gets overwhelmed by emotions, and is often unaware of the situations that trigger emotional outbreaks.

Problem Solving – The adult scoring High on this scale perceives the above named child or teen does not believe that he/she, or the family, has the ability to solve problems they encounter, or will stick together enough to solve problems that cause the family stress.

GRAND TOTAL – The adult scoring High on the total of all four scales perceives the above named child or teen does not have the coping skills to manage the stress encountered; blames others; does not communicate well; demonstrates unhealthy emotions; and has trouble solving problems.

Family Change & Crisis Workbook

Family Stress Scale
Family Score Totals

For each of the items on the scales, insert the person's name completing the scale, and transfer each person's scale on one line below. This form can be helpful in allowing family members to compare their own results.

Scale 1 Name (Child's/Teen's Scale)	Score Avoiding Blame	Score Commun- ication	Score Managing Emotions	Score Problem Solving	TOTAL SCORE
(example) John	12	15	8	16	51

Scale 2 Name (Child's/Teen's Perception of Adult Scale)	Score Avoiding Blame	Score Commun- ication	Score Managing Emotions	Score Problem Solving	TOTAL SCORE

Scale 3 Name (Adult's Identity Scale)	Score Avoiding Blame	Score Commun- ication	Score Managing Emotions	Score Problem Solving	TOTAL SCORE

Scale 4 Name (Adult's Perception of Child's/Teen's Scale)	Score Avoiding Blame	Score Commun- ication	Score Managing Emotions	Score Problem Solving	TOTAL SCORE

Family Stress

Unhealthy Ways to Manage Stress

Many family members will turn to unhealthy ways of managing the stress of a family change. For the items that follow, describe why you use it, how you think it helps, and how you can overcome it.

Unhealthy Ways to Manage Stress	Why I Use this Method	How You Think It Helps	How I Can Overcome It
Smoke			
Drink alcohol			
Over-eat or Under-eat			
Watch excessive amounts of television			
Over-use a cell phone, computer, or other technology			
Withdraw from friends and family			
Withdraw from activities			
Use illegal substances			
Sleep too much			
Other			

The Trouble with Lying

Everyone knows that lying is wrong, yet people still do it for many reasons. In many crisis situations, people lie. Lies include telling half-truths, stretching the truth, omitting certain facts, failing to correct a misconception, and not telling any part of the truth at all.

In the spaces that follow, identify the people in your family (including yourself) who lie, leading up to, and during, the crisis your family has been experiencing.

A Family Member I Think is Lying	Reasons I Think This Person Lies	How This Affects Me	How This Affects Other Family Members
Example: Me	I don't want to get into trouble when I call my Dad.	Mom finds out and she's furious that I didn't tell her.	Mom is hurt because she says she wouldn't have minded if I had told the truth. And she gets angry at Dad and they argue!

What can you and/or other family members do to regain trust amongst each other?

_____

_____

_____

Family Stress

Learn to Forgive

It is helpful to accept the fact that we all live in an imperfect world and that people make mistakes. It helps to let go of anger and resentments. Negative thinking stops you from achieving something you want, makes you feel worse, and adds negativity to your life. Negativity subtracts from our energy. Free yourself from negative energy by forgiving and moving on.

In the spaces that follow, identify the people you blame for the changes your family is experiencing.

A family member I hope to forgive is …	The reasons I will try to forgive is …	This will help me, the person, and the family by …

What is so difficult about forgiving other people?

_____

_____

One way to forgive is … to forgive … but not forget the lessons it taught me.

_____

_____

Fight Fairly

All relationships involve some disagreements and conflicts. Strong relationships that practice good family stress management, talking conflicts out, trying to resolve it, and, if necessary agreeing to disagree. It is important that all members of your family learn these skills.

Some tips:
- Start your sentences with "I" rather than "You." For example, rather than attacking and saying "You're jealous and immature," start with, "I feel hurt when you question me about my previous relationships."
- Avoid generalizations such as "You always..." or "You never..."
- Focus on the issue at hand.
- Listen to what is being said rather than about what you will say next. Tuning into a family member's verbal and visual cues is important.
- Avoid cheap shots, blaming, criticizing, and the use of foul language.

Now you try. Think about a present situation with a member of your family with whom you can use this skill.

_____
_____
_____

Now, using the tips above, write out a script of something you'd like to say to this family member, and imagine what the responses might be.

_____
_____
_____
_____
_____
_____
_____
_____
_____
_____

Family Stress

Family Enjoyment

When going through changes, family members often focus too much on the crises in their lives and forget about enjoying time together. Think about family you enjoy spending time with, and others you wish you enjoyed more.

I have fun with _____ by …

I would like to have fun with _____ by …

When I'm with _____ we laugh a lot!

I would like to laugh more with _____ by …

I enjoy _____'s company when …

I would like to enjoy _____'s company by …

I feel grateful for what I have when I'm with _____ because …

I do not have a feeling of gratitude when I'm with _____ because …

Even when things are tough for me, _____ can make me smile by …

When things are tough for me, I wish _____ would …

With my whole family, I have fun when …

I wish our family could _____

_____

_____

Reducing Stress

One way to help reduce the stress occurring in the family is to engage in a variety of coping strategies (with family members or alone). In the spaces below, identify those activities.

Activities	With My Family	Myself
Relaxation		
Exercise		
Sports		
Music		
TV / Movies		
Games, Cards, Videos, etc.		
Outdoors / Nature		
Laughter		
Other		
Other		

Support

It is important to develop a support system within the family, as well as within the community. Think about how you can develop greater support within your family and within the community.

How can family members (list them) support you better?	How can you support family members (list them) better?
What support services are available for you in your community?	**What trusted friends are available to support you?**

Writing a Letter

Write a letter about the change you and your family are experiencing or have experienced. Describe how this change is affecting your life and the lives of those around you. Acknowledge the emotions you are feeling.

I, _____, now accept that a major change
    (Your Name)

has occurred in our family. I have been feeling _____

_____

_____

_____

about the change. I am working to feel better about myself and my situation.

This change has affected me in many ways: _____

_____

_____

_____

This change has also affected the members of my family in my life in the following ways:

_____

_____

_____

_____

I see the change as an opportunity for …

_____

_____

_____

_____

Family Stress

What is in My Control and What Isn't?

Many things in life are beyond our control – particularly the behavior of other people. Rather than stressing out over them, focus on the things you can control such as the way you choose to react to problems.

Things I Cannot Control	Things I Can Control
EXAMPLE: We moved away.	I am noticing some advantages of the move.

My Fears about Our Future

Many family members have fears about how family changes will affect their own future. In the spaces that follow, explore your fears about your future.

My Fears about My Future	Is it Realistic?	What Can I Do About It?
1.		
2.		
3.		
4.		

Who can you talk with about each of these fears?

1. _____
2. _____
3. _____
4. _____

Appreciation

Every member of a family is unique and it is important to recognize what you appreciate about each one. In the spaces that follow, identify your family members and describe something you appreciate about each of them. (Even if you think there is nothing you appreciate about a particular person, think hard. You might find something!)

Family Member	What I Appreciate About This Person	How I Will Let This Person Know What I Appreciate

Playing the Blame Game

How you react to stressful family times says a lot about whether you will cope effectively or fall apart under the stress. Blaming other family members is a fairly common reaction, but it won't solve the family problem. Think about the people you currently blame for the family crisis, why you blame them, and what might be their side of the story.

A family member I blame for the change is …	I blame this person because …	This person's side of the story is …

Family Stress

Playing the Blame Game

Try to view stressful situations in a more positive way. Rather than seeing each change or problem your family has as negative, try and look at it in a different way. How you view the change can be important in how well you are able to deal with it. Remember, doing the same thing all of the time yields the same results.

Answer the following questions about the change you are experiencing.

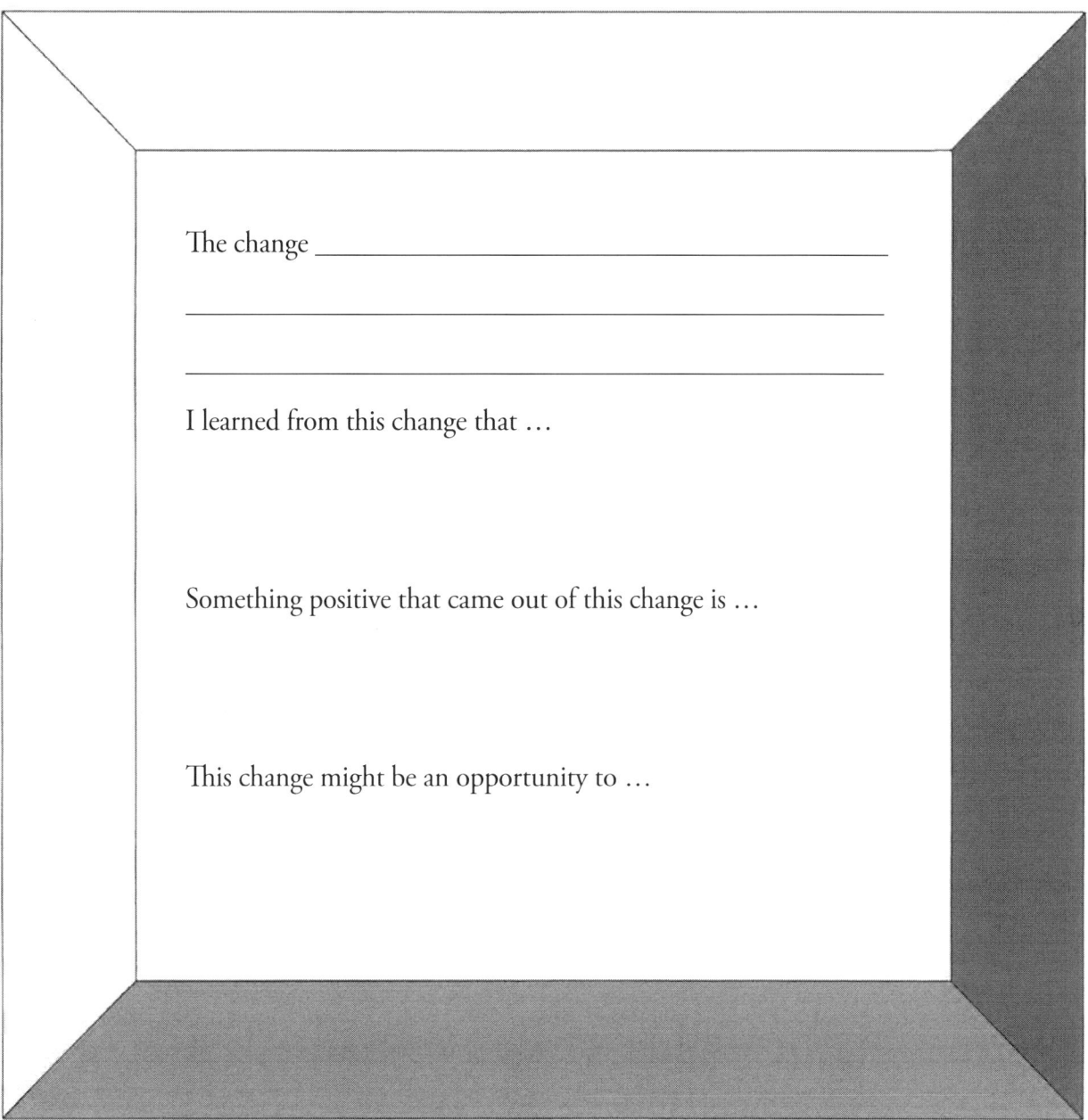

The change _____

_____

_____

I learned from this change that …

Something positive that came out of this change is …

This change might be an opportunity to …

"We cannot solve our problems with the same thinking we used when we created them."

~Albert Einstein

New Routines

*When families are facing change and stress, they usually
need to establish ways of revising family habits and routines to accommodate the change.*

*Think about how the change has affected yourself and members of the family,
and identify ways that you and your family can establish new routines and habits
to cope with the change.*

Which past family routines have been disrupted because of the change?

How has this disruption affected you?

How has the disruption affected other members of your family?

What are some new positive routines that have been established?

What are some new negative routines that have been established?

With whom can you talk to discuss your feelings about the negative routines?

Family Stress

Four-Step Family Problem Solving

A great place to start dealing with change is to work toward solving the problem.

Try this Four-Step Problem-Solving System:

Step 1: Problem Identification and Agreement

Without placing blame, try to get other family members to agree on the problem.

State the problem to be solved: _____

_____

_____

_____

_____

Step 2: Creating Options

What are some of the things that you believe can be done to resolve this issue? (Include yourself!)

Family Members	What This Person Can Do Within Reason
_____	_____
_____	_____
_____	_____
_____	_____
_____	_____
_____	_____
_____	_____
_____	_____

(Continued on the next page.)

Four-Step Family Problem Solving *(Continued)*

Step 3: Evaluate and Eliminate Obstacles

Evaluate what YOU are willing to try.

I am willing to try …

_____

_____

_____

_____

I want to overcome these obstacles that I can control …

_____

_____

_____

_____

Step 4: Identify Needed Resources

What is needed by family members to make this happen?

_____

_____

_____

_____

_____

_____

_____

_____

CHAPTER IV

Family Resilience

For the Facilitator

Explanation of the four scales in this chapter

As the facilitator, you may choose any combination of assessments that will work for each of the particular families with whom you are working.

You may choose to use one scale or all of them,
depending on the make-up of the family and the number of people in the family.

Photocopy as many of each as needed.

1. **One for each child/teen** to identity personal feelings

2. **One for each child/teen** to identify perceptions of adults' feelings

3. **One for each adult** to identity personal feelings

4. **One for each adult** to identify perceptions of children's or teens' feelings

**You will need to photocopy the corresponding
Introduction and Directions
for each scale you administer.**

Chapter IV – *Family Resilience* Skills

These skills are behavioral objectives which family members will meet as they engage in the assessments and guided self-exploration activities.

Children/Teens
Identify their own thoughts, feelings and behaviors related to their family's resilience and their perceptions of one or more adults' thoughts, feelings and behaviors in the family setting by responding to six prompts in each of these categories:
  Family Bonding
  Build Self-Esteem
  Take Care of Self
  Positive Support

Adults
Identify their own thoughts, feelings and behaviors related to their family's resilience and their perceptions of one or more children/teens' thoughts, feelings and behaviors in the family setting by responding to five prompts in the above listed categories.

All Family Members
- *Assess Family Resilience* scores as low, moderate or high on the *Scale Profile Interpretation*.
- Identify their scores' meanings based on the *Scale Profile Interpretation* and *Scale Descriptions*.
- Compare their perceptions by entering scores onto a *Family Resilience Scale*.
- State efforts self and other members can contribute four or more types of chores.
- Identify own and members' strengths, and their effects on self and others.
- Describe three positive perspectives regarding a family change.
- Write three positive personal and/or family mottos.
- Identify five or more family activities their effects on self and others.
- List meal-time routines for one week and ways to improve togetherness.
- Document ways to encourage each member regarding individual strengths.
- Share daily reminders of ways to show appreciation for each member.
- Give examples of kindness toward members, then examine the results.
- Document ways individual and family interests are encouraged and shared.
- Describe a recent family special event, members' strengths and contributions.
- Depict self with thought bubbles describing a current situation.
- Estimate the current situation's relative importance from a long-term perspective.
- Describe qualities respected in members and self, and ways respect is demonstrated.
- Summarize six aspects of the family's resilience, through sentence completions.

Family Resilience Scale
Introduction & Directions

Families today experience an unbelievable number of changes and problems that have the potential to produce stress and crisis. Rather than focusing on the deficiencies of families, it is more productive to focus on how families build resiliency (the ability to rebound from adversity, to be strengthened and to be more resourceful).

This scale can help you explore your and your family's ability to respond to stress, be strengthened, and become resilient because of it. This assessment contains 24 statements. Read each of the statements and decide how descriptive the statement is of you. In each of the choices listed, circle the number of your response on the line to the right of each statement.

Examples

Scale # 1 and # 3 (Individual's responses)

In the following example, the circled number 3 indicates that the statement is a somewhat descriptive of the person completing the scale.

4 = Very Descriptive   3 = Somewhat Descriptive   2 = A Little Descriptive   1 = Not At All

Within my family ...

I do many things together with them . . . . 4 . . . .(3.). . . 2 1

Scale # 2 and # 4: (Individual's perceptions)

In the following example, the circled number 1 indicates the person who is completing the scale perceives that it is not at all descriptive about the other family member.

Within my family ...

I do many things together with them . . . . 4 . . . . . 3 . . . . . 2 . . . .(1)

This is not a test and there are no right or wrong answers. Do not spend too much time thinking about your answers. Your initial response will be the most true for you. Be sure to respond to every statement.

(Turn to the next page and begin.)

Family Change & Crisis Workbook

SCALE #1
Child's/Teen's *Family Resilience*

Child's/Teen's Name _____ Date _____

4 = Very Descriptive   **3 = Somewhat Descriptive**   **2 = A Little Descriptive**   **1 = Not At All**

Within my family ...

I do many things together with them	4 .... 3 .... 2 1
I have times when I talk with a family member about the changes in my life	4 .... 3 .... 2 1
I laugh a lot with them	4 .... 3 .... 2 1
I do not withdraw from other(s)	4 .... 3 .... 2 1
I help other(s) through rough times	4 .... 3 .... 2 1
I play games and sports with them	4 .... 3 .... 2 1

I. TOTAL = _____

Within my family ...

I tell others what I appreciate about them	4 .... 3 .... 2 1
Other(s) tell me what they appreciate about me	4 .... 3 .... 2 1
I compliment others	4 .... 3 .... 2 1
Other(s) compliment me	4 .... 3 .... 2 1
I try to help others look on the bright side regardless of the situation	4 .... 3 .... 2 1
I like to encourage other(s)	4 .... 3 .... 2 1

II. TOTAL = _____

Within my family ...

I pay attention to my own needs	4 .... 3 .... 2 1
I find ways to relax when I'm stressed	4 .... 3 .... 2 1
I exercise	4 .... 3 .... 2 1
I make sure I eat in a healthy way	4 .... 3 .... 2 1
I get enough sleep	4 .... 3 .... 2 1
I pay attention to my personal hygiene	4 .... 3 .... 2 1

III. TOTAL = _____

Within and outside of my family ...

I support other(s)	4 .... 3 .... 2 1
I am able to rely on other(s) for help when needed	4 .... 3 .... 2 1
I stay involved in outside activities	4 .... 3 .... 2 1
I have support systems within the family	4 .... 3 .... 2 1
I know who to contact for my various supportive needs	4 .... 3 .... 2 1
I have supportive people outside of the family	4 .... 3 .... 2 1

IV. TOTAL = _____

Family Resilience

SCALE #1
Child's/Teen's *Family Resilience*
Scale Scoring Directions

Child's/Teen's Name _____ Date _____

This scale you just completed is designed to measure how well you are building resilience to manage your present stress as well as the stress that might occur in the future.
For each of the items on the previous page, count the scores you circled.
Put that total on the line marked TOTAL at the end of each section.
Then add your four scores to find your GRAND TOTAL.

      I   Fun and Bonding   Total = _____
     II   Build Self-Esteem   Total = _____
    III   Take Care of Self   Total = _____
    IV   Positive Support   Total = _____
                 GRAND TOTAL = _____

Scale Profile Interpretation

Individual Score	Grand Total	Result	Indications
6 - 11	24 - 48	Low	Low scores indicate that you are not doing all of the things you could do to build resiliency.
12 - 18	49 - 72	Moderate	Moderate scores indicate that you are doing some of the things necessary to build resiliency.
19 - 24	73 - 96	High	High scores indicate that you are doing well in building your resiliency.

Individual Scale Descriptions

Fun and Bonding – The child or teen scoring Low on this scale is not doing enough enjoyable activities in order to bond with other members of the family.
Build Self-Esteem – The child or teen scoring Low on this scale is not doing very much to build other family members self-esteem.
Take Care of Self – The child or teen scoring Low on this scale is not doing enough to take care of self.
Positive Support – The child or teen scoring Low on this scale does not have enough support either within the family or outside of the family, or both.

GRAND TOTAL – The child or teen scoring Low on the total of all four scales needs to gain many new and different skills to become resilient within self and within the family.

SCALE #2
Child's/Teen's Perception of an Adult's *Family Resilience* Scale

Child's/Teen's Name _____

Adult's Name _____ Date _____

4 = Very Descriptive   3 = Somewhat Descriptive   2 = A Little Descriptive   1 = Not At All

Within my family, this adult ...

does many things together with me	4......3......2......1
talks with me about the changes	4......3......2......1
laughs a lot with me	4......3......2......1
does not withdraw from me	4......3......2......1
helps me through rough times	4......3......2......1
plays games and sports with me	4......3......2......1

I. TOTAL = _____

Within my family, this adult ...

expresses appreciation to other family members	4......3......2......1
expresses appreciation to me	4......3......2......1
compliments others	4......3......2......1
compliments me	4......3......2......1
tries to help others look on the bright side regardless of the situation	4......3......2......1
tries to help me look on the bright side regardless of the situation	4......3......2......1

II. TOTAL = _____

This adult ...

pays attention to personal needs	4......3......2......1
finds ways to relax when stressed	4......3......2......1
exercises	4......3......2......1
eats in a healthy way	4......3......2......1
gets enough sleep	4......3......2......1
pays attention to personal hygiene	4......3......2......1

III. TOTAL = _____

Within and outside of my family, this adult ...

supports other(s)	4......3......2......1
is able to rely on other(s) for help when needed	4......3......2......1
stays involved in outside activities	4......3......2......1
has support systems within the family	4......3......2......1
knows who to contact for various supportive needs	4......3......2......1
has supportive people outside of the family	4......3......2......1

IV. TOTAL = _____

Family Resilience

SCALE #2
Child's/Teen's Perception of an Adult's *Family Resilience* Scale Scoring Directions

Child's/Teen's Name _____

Adult's Name _____ Date _____

This scale you just completed is designed to measure how well you are building resilience to manage your present stress as well as the stress that might occur in the future.
For each of the items on the previous page, count the scores you circled.
Put that total on the line marked TOTAL at the end of each section.
Then add your four scores to find your GRAND TOTAL.

I	Fun and Bonding	Total = _____
II	Build Self-Esteem	Total = _____
III	Take Care of Self	Total = _____
IV	Positive Support	Total = _____
	GRAND TOTAL =	_____

Scale Profile Interpretation

Individual Score	Grand Total	Result	Indications
6 - 11	24 - 48	Low	Low scores indicate that you perceive the above named adult is not doing all of the things needed to build resiliency.
12 - 18	49 - 72	Moderate	Moderate scores indicate that you perceive the above named adult is doing some of the things necessary to build resiliency.
19 - 24	73 - 96	High	High scores indicate that you perceive the above named adult is doing what is needed to build resiliency.

Individual Scale Descriptions

Fun and Bonding – Low scores indicate that you perceive the above named adult is not doing enough enjoyable activities to bond as a family.
Build Self-Esteem – Low scores indicate that you perceive the above named adult is not doing enough to build others' self-esteem.
Take Care of Self – Low scores indicate that you perceive the above named adult is not taking care of self to build resiliency.
Positive Support – Low scores indicate that you perceive the above named adult is not doing enough to gain support.

GRAND TOTAL – Low scores indicate that you perceive the above named adult needs to gain many different skills to become resilient within self and within the family.

Family Change & Crisis Workbook

SCALE #3
Adult's *Family Resilience*

Adult's Name _____ Date _____

4 = Very Descriptive   3 = Somewhat Descriptive   2 = A Little Descriptive   1 = Not At All

Within my family ...

I do many things together with them	4 . . . 3 . . . 2 . . . 1
I have times when I talk with a family member about the changes in my life	4 . . . 3 . . . 2 . . . 1
I laugh a lot with them	4 . . . 3 . . . 2 . . . 1
I do not withdraw from other(s)	4 . . . 3 . . . 2 . . . 1
I help other(s) through rough times	4 . . . 3 . . . 2 . . . 1
I play games and sports with them	4 . . . 3 . . . 2 . . . 1

I. TOTAL = _____

Within my family ...

I tell others what I appreciate about them	4 . . . 3 . . . 2 . . . 1
Other(s) tell me what they appreciate about me	4 . . . 3 . . . 2 . . . 1
I compliment others	4 . . . 3 . . . 2 . . . 1
Other(s) compliment me	4 . . . 3 . . . 2 . . . 1
I try to help others look on the bright side regardless of the situation	4 . . . 3 . . . 2 . . . 1
I like to encourage other(s)	4 . . . 3 . . . 2 . . . 1

II. TOTAL = _____

Within my family ...

I pay attention to my own needs	4 . . . 3 . . . 2 . . . 1
I find ways to relax when I'm stressed	4 . . . 3 . . . 2 . . . 1
I exercise	4 . . . 3 . . . 2 . . . 1
I make sure I eat in a healthy way	4 . . . 3 . . . 2 . . . 1
I get enough sleep	4 . . . 3 . . . 2 . . . 1
I pay attention to my personal hygiene	4 . . . 3 . . . 2 . . . 1

III. TOTAL = _____

Within and outside of my family ...

I support other(s)	4 . . . 3 . . . 2 . . . 1
I am able to rely on other(s) for help when needed	4 . . . 3 . . . 2 . . . 1
I stay involved in outside activities	4 . . . 3 . . . 2 . . . 1
I have support systems within the family	4 . . . 3 . . . 2 . . . 1
I know who to contact for my various supportive needs	4 . . . 3 . . . 2 . . . 1
I have supportive people outside of the family	4 . . . 3 . . . 2 . . . 1

IV. TOTAL = _____

Family Resilience

SCALE #3
Adult's *Family* Resilience
Scale Scoring Directions

Adult's Name _____ Date _____

This scale you just completed is designed to measure how well you are building resilience to manage your present stress as well as the stress that might occur in the future.
For each of the items on the previous page, count the scores you circled.
Put that total on the line marked TOTAL at the end of each section.
Then add your four scores to find your GRAND TOTAL.

I	Fun and Bonding	Total = _____
II	Build Self-Esteem	Total = _____
III	Take Care of Self	Total = _____
IV	Positive Support	Total = _____
	GRAND TOTAL =	_____

Scale Profile Interpretation

Individual Score	Grand Total	Result	Indications
6 - 11	24 - 48	Low	Low scores indicate that your family is not doing all of the things to build resiliency.
12 - 18	49 - 72	Moderate	Moderate scores indicate that your family is doing some of the things necessary to build resiliency.
19 - 24	73 - 96	High	High scores indicate that your family is doing things to build resiliency.

Individual Scale Descriptions

Fun and Bonding – The adult scoring Low on this scale is not doing enough enjoyable activities in order to bond with other members of the family.
Build Self-Esteem – The adult scoring Low on this scale is not doing very much to build other family members self-esteem.
Take Care of Self – The adult scoring Low on this scale is not doing enough to take care of self.
Positive Support – The adult scoring Low on this scale does not have enough support either within the family or outside of the family, or both.

GRAND TOTAL – The adult scoring Low on the total of all four scales needs to gain many new and different skills to become resilient within self and within the family.

Family Change & Crisis Workbook

SCALE #4
Adult's Perception of a Child's/Teen's *Family Resilience* Scale

Adult's Name _____

Child's/Teen's Name _____ Date _____

4 = Very Descriptive   3 = Somewhat Descriptive   2 = A Little Descriptive   1 = Not At All

Within my family, this adult …

does many things together with me . . . . 4 . . . . . 3 . . . . . 2 1
talks with me about the changes. . . . . 4 . . . . . 3 . . . . . 2 1
laughs a lot with me . . . . 4 . . . . . 3 . . . . . 2 1
does not withdraw from me . . . . 4 . . . . . 3 . . . . . 2 1
helps me through rough times . . . . 4 . . . . . 3 . . . . . 2 1
plays games and sports with me . . . . 4 . . . . . 3 . . . . . 2 1

I. TOTAL = _____

Within my family, this adult …

expresses appreciation to other family members . . . . 4 . . . . . 3 . . . . . 2 1
expresses appreciation to me. . . . . 4 . . . . . 3 . . . . . 2 1
compliments others . . . . 4 . . . . . 3 . . . . . 2 1
compliments me. . . . . 4 . . . . . 3 . . . . . 2 1
tries to help others look on the bright side regardless of the situation . . . . 4 . . . . . 3 . . . . . 2 1
tries to help me look on the bright side regardless of the situation . . . . . 4 . . . . . 3 . . . . . 2 1

II. TOTAL = _____

This adult …

pays attention to personal needs . . . . 4 . . . . . 3 . . . . . 2 1
finds ways to relax when stressed. . . . . 4 . . . . . 3 . . . . . 2 1
exercises . . . . 4 . . . . . 3 . . . . . 2 1
eats in a healthy way. . . . . 4 . . . . . 3 . . . . . 2 1
gets enough sleep . . . . 4 . . . . . 3 . . . . . 2 1
pays attention to personal hygiene . . . . 4 . . . . . 3 . . . . . 2 1

III. TOTAL = _____

Within and outside of my family, this adult …

supports other(s). . . . . 4 . . . . . 3 . . . . . 2 1
is able to rely on other(s) for help when needed . . . . 4 . . . . . 3 . . . . . 2 1
stays involved in outside activities. . . . . 4 . . . . . 3 . . . . . 2 1
has support systems within the family . . . . 4 . . . . . 3 . . . . . 2 1
knows who to contact for various supportive needs . . . . 4 . . . . . 3 . . . . . 2 1
has supportive people outside of the family . . . . 4 . . . . . 3 . . . . . 2 1

IV. TOTAL = _____

Family Resilience

SCALE #4
Adult's Perception of a Child's/Teen's *Family Resilience* Scale Scoring Directions

Adult's Name _____

Child's/Teen's Name _____ Date _____

This scale you just completed is designed to measure how well you are building resilience to manage your present stress as well as the stress that might occur in the future.
For each of the items on the previous page, count the scores you circled.
Put that total on the line marked TOTAL at the end of each section.
Then add your four scores to find your GRAND TOTAL.

I	Fun and Bonding	Total = _____
II	Build Self-Esteem	Total = _____
III	Take Care of Self	Total = _____
IV	Positive Support	Total = _____
	GRAND TOTAL =	_____

Scale Profile Interpretation

Individual Score	Grand Total	Result	Indications
6 - 11	24 - 48	Low	Low scores indicate that you perceive the above named child or teen is not doing all of the things needed to build resiliency.
12 - 18	49 - 72	Moderate	Moderate scores indicate that you perceive the above named child or teen is doing some of the things necessary to build resiliency.
19 - 24	73 - 96	High	High scores indicate that you perceive the above named child or teen is doing what is needed to build resiliency.

Individual Scale Descriptions

Fun and Bonding – Low scores indicate that you perceive the above named child or teen is not doing enough enjoyable activities to bond as a family.
Build Self-Esteem – Low scores indicate that you perceive the above named child or teen is not doing enough to build others' self-esteem.
Take Care of Self – Low scores indicate that you perceive the above named child or teen is not taking care of self to build resiliency.
Positive Support – Low scores indicate that you perceive the above named child or teen is not doing enough to gain support.

GRAND TOTAL – Low scores indicate that you perceive the above named child or teen needs to gain many different skills to become resilient within self and within the family.

Family Resilience Scale
Family Score Totals

For each of the items on the scales, insert the person's name completing the scale, and transfer each person's scale on one line below. This form can be helpful in allowing family members to compare their own results.

Scale 1 Name (Child's/Teen's Scale)	Score Fun & Bonding	Score Build Self-Esteem	Score Take Care of Self	Score Provide Support	TOTAL SCORE
(example) John	20	18	12	6	56

Scale 2 Name (Child's/Teen's Perception of Adult Scale)	Score Fun & Bonding	Score Build Self-Esteem	Score Take Care of Self	Score Provide Support	TOTAL SCORE

Scale 3 Name (Adult's Identity Scale)	Score Fun & Bonding	Score Build Self-Esteem	Score Take Care of Self	Score Provide Support	TOTAL SCORE

Scale 4 Name (Adult's Perception of Child's/Teen's Scale)	Score Fun & Bonding	Score Build Self-Esteem	Score Take Care of Self	Score Provide Support	TOTAL SCORE

Family Resilience

The Family That Works Together

Completing simple household chores as a family can help families build resiliency to overcome future stress. Working together offers the family time to communicate, lightens the load for individual family members, and lets individuals build skills and feel a sense of belonging, and contribution to the household. Think about some of the chores that you and others in your family do.

Family Chores	How I Contribute	How Others Contribute
Inside the house		
Outdoors		
Shopping		
Repairs		
Other		

What else could you do to help?

_____

_____

What else could others do to help?

_____

_____

Family Strengths

In each line of the table that follows, identify a family member, state this person's personal strengths, how this strength affects you, and then how it affects other family members.
Start with yourself!

Family Member	Strength	How This Strength Affects You	How it Affects Other Family Members
EXAMPLE: Grandma	She is very wise, and very calming.	She is always there for me and I feel better after talking with her.	Some family members agree with me and some think it's annoying when she gives advice.

Optimistic People

Regardless of the type of change optimistic people are experiencing, they are able to look at the bright side, and at the same time, look at the situation realistically. Families whose members strive to see the brighter side of life tend to be the most resilient in the face of change.

Think about ways you can see the change in your life with a positive perspective (way of looking at something).

Example: CHANGE: *We moved to a new city with a new family member.*
Perspective 1. *I will learn about a new city.*
Perspective 2. *This is an opportunity to make new friends*
Perspective 3. *There are different types of activities to become involved in.*

The CHANGE: _____

_____

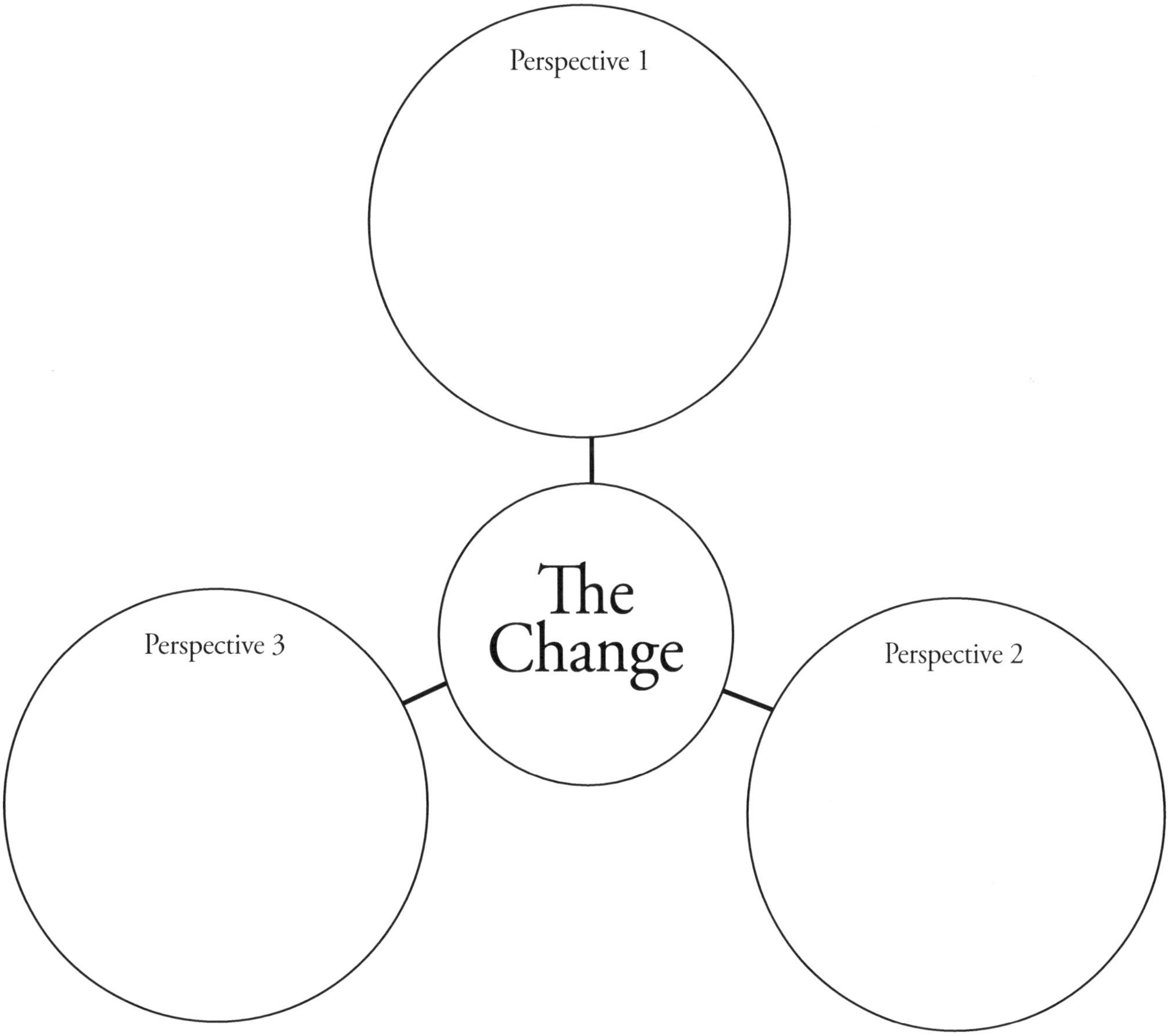

- Perspective 1
- The Change
- Perspective 2
- Perspective 3

Positive Mottos

Mottos are short sentences or phrases that show beliefs or purposes that are meant to stand for something and to guide us.

Write what you believe are some of your POSITIVE personal or family mottos.

EXAMPLE: "I'll be OK no matter what." or "Our family is as solid as a rock."

Family Resilience

Learn to Forgive

It is helpful to accept the fact that we all live in an imperfect world and that people make mistakes. It helps to let go of anger and resentments. Negative thinking stops you from achieving something you want, makes you feel worse, and adds negativity to your life. Negativity subtracts from our energy. Free yourself from negative energy by forgiving and moving on.

In the spaces that follow, identify the people you blame for the changes your family is experiencing.

What We Do As a Family	How This Affects Me	How This Affects Other Members of My Family
Meals		
Entertainment		
Outings		
Homework		
Community		
Other		
Other		
Other		

Share Meals Together

Mealtime is often hectic with individuals having different work and activity schedules. However, mealtime (even if it's not every meal, every day) is a great time to catch up with each person's happenings. In the spaces that follow, identify your typical meal routines, and then consider whether it works well, or if not, how it can be better.

Days of the Week	Our Meal Routine	Does This Work Well?	How Can it Work Better?
Monday			
Tuesday			
Wednesday			
Thursday			
Friday			
Saturday			
Sunday			

Family Resilience

enCOURAGEment

Family members who praise and encourage other family members are able to make their day! Sometimes it takes COURAGE to enCOURAGE someone, but you'll usually find that when you do, you will feel good about yourself, too!

Family Member	Each Family Member's Strengths	How I Can Encourage This Person
Example: Aunt Jane	KINDNESS - She is so kind to me!	When she says something kind to me I can thank her and tell her how much it means to me.

The word Gestalt means "The whole is greater than the sum of its parts."

Your family can be an even stronger unit than the individual strengths of each family member if you all contribute and encourage each other.

Daily Reminders

One way to remain strong as a family is to provide daily reminders of your appreciation and love. These daily reminders can be related to your positive feelings about other family members, expressions about your commitment and appreciation, and your affection for them.

Family Members	My Positive Feelings about This Person	How I Show It
EXAMPLE: Step-Mom	She treats me the same as she does her biological children. That means so much to me.	I sometimes go up to her and give her a hug. She asks what it's for and I tell her it's because I love her!

How does it feel to show and/or express positive emotions about members of your family?

Family Resilience

Kindness Re-examined

Showing kindness toward family members can help develop resiliency. Kindness does not cost money. It can just be shown with thoughtfulness and consideration. Families that make kindness a habit tend to be much more resilient in times of change and stress.

In the first two columns, identify some of the ways you can be kind to family members.
In one week, come back to this page and fill in the third column.

Family Members	**Ways I Will Be Kind**	*(In one week, fill in)* **Examining the Results**
EXAMPLE: Foster sister, Jan	I'll offer to help her with homework, though she's not very friendly.	At first she said "no," but then she let me help. We get along much better.

Interests

Family members need to have their own individual interests, things they enjoy doing. In a family unit, it is gratifying when others take an interest in what they are doing, but still respect the fact that they like to do these things alone or with their friends.

My Interests and My Family Members' Interests	How I/We Share This Interest With Our Family.	Who Encourages Me? How Do I Encourage Others?
EXAMPLE of My Interests: I am a member of a chess club	I come home from a game and tell people who are interested how I did.	My brother Bob and sister Terry always ask about details.
EXAMPLE of My Family Member's Interests: Kathy likes to exercise.	I don't like to exercise and she always tells me I should! She tells others!	I don't encourage her. Others do.

Family Resilience

Family Events

A special activity can be as complex as a family vacation or as simple as a trip to the local park or a family movie night. Planning the activity as a family unit is half the fun, especially when each family member contributes to making it a successful and enjoyable occasion.

Our last family event was _____

List All Family Members	This Person's Strength Related to the Event	This Person's Contribution (or Not)
EXAMPLE: my Aunt Sally	She does research on the internet.	She found us a movie we all agreed on!
EXAMPLE: my Dad	He's a great driver.	He was tired and didn't drive.

How does including everyone in the event make it special?

_____

_____

Looking at the Big Picture

What is a current stressful family situation? _____

In the picture frame provided, draw a picture of yourself thinking about this family situation. You can put in thought bubbles of what you are thinking.

Ask yourself how important this situation will be in the long run. Will it matter in a month? A year? Is it really worth getting upset over? If the answer is no, focus your time and energy elsewhere.

Family Resilience

Respect

Respect is a feeling of admiration, and treating people that way. Identify below what you respect about each member of your family, and how you do and can show this respect!

Family Member	What I Respect About this Person	How I Show this Respect	How I Can Show More Respect
EXAMPLE: My daughter Julie	She helps in every way she can, and always tries to keep the peace in the family.	I thank her.	I can give her "I love you" notes and cards to remind her of my appreciation.

What do you think members of your family respect about you?

_____

_____

_____

Family Change & Crisis Workbook

Our Family's Strengths

Your individual family members each have significant strengths.
However, your family as a unit also has significant strengths. Identify your family strengths.

Our greatest strength as a family unit is _____
_____
_____
_____

Three things we enjoy doing together are …

    1) _____

    2) _____

    3) _____

We are at our best when _____
_____
_____

As a family, we never _____
_____
_____

As a family, we always _____
_____
_____

When the going gets tough, we _____
_____
_____

Family Resilience

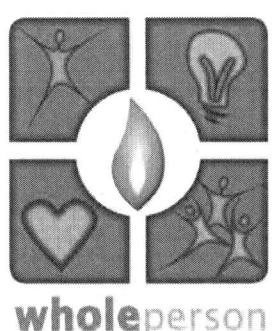

Whole Person Associates is the leading publisher of training resources for professionals who empower people to create and maintain healthy lifestyles. Our creative resources will help you work effectively with your clients in the areas of stress management, wellness promotion, mental health and life skills.

Please visit us at our web site: **www.wholeperson.com**. You can check out our entire line of products, place an order, request our print catalog, and sign up for our monthly special notifications.

Whole Person Associates
800-247-6789